ANCHOR BOOKS

NO TWO PEOPLE ARE THE SAME

Edited by

Steve Twelvetree

First published in Great Britain in 2004 by
ANCHOR BOOKS
Remus House,
Coltsfoot Drive,
Peterborough, PE2 9JX
Telephone (01733) 898102

SB ISBN 1 84418 382 3

FOREWORD

Anchor Books is a small press, established in 1992, with the aim of promoting readable poetry to as wide an audience as possible.

We hope to establish an outlet for writers of poetry who may have struggled to see their work in print.

The poems presented here have been selected from many entries, and as always editing proved to be a difficult task.

I trust this selection will delight and please the authors and all those who enjoy reading poetry.

Steve Twelvetree
Editor

CONTENTS

BLUE EYES BRIGHT

A baby girl is born to the night,
All blonde hair and blue eyes bright,
Her heart is that of finest crystal,
Broken from the birth.
Her mother she's a game to play,
Her father not a lot to say,
Her brother he has little more,
Than years ahead of she.

She grows into a teenage dream,
She wants for more than what has been,
Takes a chance to run her way,
But always on the coming day.
Now her eyes are jaded green,
Now her story's something seen,
A thousand times, a thousand ways,
She is no original display.

Though the story's old as time,
The character leading is the original kind,
The way they move, perform and speak,
The program different every week.
So try she will to be a star,
To shine a light to people far,
To bring back home the message true,
She is she and you are you.

It will matter not when rain flows free,
When everybody wants to disagree,
When the limb of change is cold and lonely,
When nothing feels all warm and homely,
She's in your heart and in your mind,
There for anyone to look and find,
She'll speak the message loud and true,
She is she and you are you.

Eleanor Mary Page-John

BLINDNESS

When I first thought of blindness,
It certainly made me feel sadness,
How can folk cope that are not sighted,
Then I heard of help for the blinded.

There are many types of illness,
With sometimes a cure for the helpless,
So progress for all those sightless,
Need never lack support by the righteous.

War with its victims, lies exposed.
How many are those so involved,
Young or old in battle fought,
Surely not forgotten as an after thought.

How luck are the blinded these days,
With help at hand in so many ways,
Dedication has ways to help the blind,
Not least with helping hand to understand.

With games like dominoes and talking books,
Large print reading books and Braille,
Then talking cassettes and music never fail,
Will make life less tedious for all.

So let's pay a tribute to those involved
With all the efforts that are entailed,
Their every bent to help any that are blind,
What a poor world without their aid.

Bill Burkitt

THOUGHTS

Sometimes I think about life
Watching the second hand tick by
Time may be eternal
But not mortality, not I

The thoughts that I have in this time
Could all just go to waste
If not for paper and pen
Easy to forget these thoughts in haste

These thoughts are now left for time to see
If for nobody else, then at least for me
To recollect and remind me
Of the man that I once used to be

Clearly legible on paper
Thoughts in time, taken from my mind
I cannot take them with me
But I can leave them behind.

Paul Frederick Clayton

FREEDOM

The valley so green
The sea so blue
What does all this mean to you

Would you for instance
Be sad if you lost
The right to be British
At a very high cost

To walk in the fields
So free and so gay
To be able to talk
Not afraid what to say

To go swimming and golfing
Football and that kind
To please yourself only
No one to bother your peace of mind

We have all this now
And we must take heed
To be too complacent
Is the first sight of greed.

Muriel Purdy

THE NANNY STATE

Here we are, in the Nanny State;
Hurry, hurry or we will be late!
(The Queen is in her palace, all sedate!)
Cap in hand, all seek a handout,
Thousands cheat; will not be found out.
Parliament, thinks up silly laws most will flout!

Grants for this, that and the other;
Special benefits for single mothers.
All, by government, financially smothered!
Waste, waste, waste, our reserves of gold,
Will there be any left, when we get old;
We must work longer, we're told!

Can't smack a child the government say;
(Is there really some other way?)
Who knows what next, on another day.
How about starting another war;
Peacetime is such a bloodless bore.
In The House of Lords, they just merely snore!

The NHS is too heavy with top brass,
Whilst with doctors, nurses - understaffed:
(Doesn't bother those of the upper class)
You can't do this, you must do that,
These the edicts, from political prats.
'God save the Queen' and that, is that!

Peter Mahoney

BALLAD OF THE FREEMAN

One night I was led through silent streets,
Through blossomed trees with aromas sweet,
By the Freeman.
On we trooped with my arm in a sling, while he would sing,
'Til we reached a wilderness in the middle of the concrete abyss,
Up we climbed past a pond with glittering ripples and trees around,
'Til we reached a hill with bushes flowering,
Up and up we climbed, the turf springy under our feet,
Without fear we explored, my pain ignored,
The crescent moon, we could see over the myriad lights of the
city streets,
Arthur's Seat looming its lion head in silhouette against the night,
We reached a dome to the stars,
We tried to get in but it was barred,
So sat down and gazed at the sky.
'The stars are little white dots in my head,' the Freeman said.
Then he climbed a tower while I watched and marvelled at his eagle's
eye view,
Then on our way back we found the track to our starting point.

William Lightheart

HE'S LEAVING HOME

For many years I faced the fact that soon this day would come,
when I would say goodbye to him, my dear untidy son.

I felt that I was ready for him to move away,
I helped him pack, I urged him on, I kept my tears at bay.

I left him there amidst the mess of cases, books and clothes,
and halfway down the motorway my tears began to flow.

His empty room when I returned was quiet, cold and bleak,
I cursed myself, these futile tears; they made me feel so weak.

For days if someone said his name, I'd feel all choked and sad,
I really did begin to think that I was going mad.

Then came the day a tiny thought came creeping in my head,
perhaps I didn't feel so bad, it surely could be said.

That maybe now I could begin to live a different life,
without the worries children bring, the troubles and the strife.

In fact I feel I have to say, now that the years have flown,
I feel a peace, a deep content like I have never known.

And in my heart this child of mine, I love so very much,
will always hold a special place that no one else can touch.

Muriel Nicola Waldt

INHUMANE ME

So just alone life I now must try to live
Sorry but have nothing more can give
My body now old and shake with cold
Pills for cramp make me feel like a tramp
When slave was trained speed and skill
British army taught 'let live' not just simple kill
Shown how to make money fast if wish to last
Brought success in past, cannot forever last.

Block my ears so no longer can hear lies
Raise eyes only to see heavy laden skies
Call now crap as one yap maybe only way
Once led village forward flush toilet did say
Trading cramped council ramp too steep
Wasted life lost wife from now rubbish heap
Private must become this land no footpath
Corruption great but big mistake all laugh.

Sorry am inhumane, have a too-fast heart
Will last years just smile make it work of art
To waste I never could now told must should
Hate not take the rubbish and still more wood
Was trained care and share for hate return love
In aviary still live my wonder once broken dove
Please don't take sides I'd rather just walk alone
Block insanity, innocence uneasiness on throne.

John J Flint

LOVE DENIED

Feeling the pain my body and mind aches.
While my heart beats it can never forsake
The dishonour, shame and self disgust,
Of our denied love, unhappiness and mistrust.

Yes, I've a reason for my melancholy and woe,
At a time when I was so proud to show
My deepest feelings and longing to share,
My life with another, who now isn't there.

It all went wrong, sad and benign,
The love we once shared, sadly declined.
Our life ended, separated we both knew,
That together our life just wasn't true.

Parting, we shared only guilt and cold,
Yet in reflection, we had so much to hold.
Togetherness over, we went our separate ways,
And alone, neither found happier days.

Now as I sit here I will ever regret,
The seven long years, since we both left.
I was such a fool, ruining my life,
Losing the love and respect of my wife.

She suffered so much pain, I never knew,
Lingering for years, heartbroken too.
Left me a letter, she'd loved me always
And didn't realise, I too felt that way.

As I look back, it is a consolation to me,
To know that some day, my sadness will flee.
The guilt I feel with the love we denied,
Will end when we're reunited on the other side.

George Carrick

THE KIRSTNIN' OF GAVIN ROBERT
(Christening of a grandson with an over-anxious mother)

She invaded the vestry on Saturday night,
to check a'thing ower for the morn,
For the kirstnin' o' Gavin, her second son,
six months since he was born.

The Baptismal font was sterilised, an scrubbit to perfection,
Gavin's broo was algipanned, a precaution 'gainst infection.

She made the meenister wash his hands,
an trim his nails forbye,
She checked his heid for dandruff,
his not to reason why.
She lectured him for ae' hale hoor,
made sure he kent full well,
She widna hae his blessed water,
she'd bile some hersel'.

An when she felt he really knew,
what exactly she's for havin',
She warned him weel, now don't forget!
Dinna breath on Gavin.

Tammy D

ORCHID OF LOVE

When hearts combine, when hearts unite
Doves of love take to flight
One true feeling, one true care
Sharing life their souls laid bare
Look to the future not the past
A love that's true will thrive and last

To be together in love and pain
All life's problems will be slain
Two people separate all alone
Together sharing love's wondrous throne

Roses may say I love you
Like words they're easy to grow
An orchid needs love and tenderness
Care, to give its best show

As love will die without passion
So will an orchid fail
Will you let me feed that passion
To let our dreams set sail?

Stuart Garrett

A GLIMPSE OF NATURE

Through sleepy eyes one views the dawn,
A lazy stretch, a gaping yawn.
Beyond the frosted windowpane
The village begins to breathe again.

The creeping glow of a golden sunrise
Makes you peer through half-closed eyes.
To glimpse through the early morning light
The splendour of nature's rare delight.

The hedgerow bathed in a ghostly whiteness
A spidery frosted, shimmering brightness.
That brings to mind a world unreal
Revealing winter's ice-cold appeal.

On the ground a slight covering of snow
Powdery and fluffy, it's enough to show
There're no footprints to and from the gate.
Revealing the milk and postman are late.

After bacon and egg, two cups of coffee
It's time to move through to the lobby.
Open the cupboard for somewhere in there
Should be a strong pair of boots to wear.

Now at last you're attired and ready
To take a stroll just nice and steady.
Out, round the corner, down the street
Calling, 'Good morning,' to those you meet.

Out of the village and up the steep hill.
Breathing quite easily enjoying the thrill.
The feeling of freedom, no worries to bear
Smiling unconsciously, life without care.

Suddenly, startlingly, a blackbird calls out
Warning the bird life that danger's about.
Out from the hedgerow and way up in a tree
He sits on a branch for all to see

Black as coal plumage, a bright orange beak,
Shouting annoyance, his voice reaching a shriek.
Disturbing the sparrows, who flit here and there
Also some blue tits who don't seem to care.

Now on the level, you're travelling quite quickly
Along past a holly bush, leaves dark and prickly.
Hawthorn hedges, elder trees and sloe
A variety of species you see as you go.

Off to the right, leads an old well-worn track
Straight into a quarry, there's the old workers' shack,
Well overgrown now with bracken and bramble
Trods here and there, a great place to ramble

In a secluded dark corner, on a large block of stone,
Lie tattered torn feathers and pieces of bone.
A possible haunt of a buzzard or falcon
It could even be the table they eat on.

Clambering along over heather and rubble,
You come to a cornfield, it's now winter stubble.
And there to the right standing proud and so clear,
Tall and majestic, a large wild red deer.

A sight of rare beauty, of power and grace
This incredible animal looks out of place.
The slightest movement, an unusual sound
Away over the fence with an effortless bound

The view now seems empty, it's gone from your vision.
A sadness at losing such a rare apparition,
But time's moving on and hunger's a pain
So retracing your steps, you head home again.

Whilst walking along certain things come to mind.
Of the peace and tranquillity that one can find
When old Mother Nature opens her heart to us all.
A reminder that nothing's too big or too small.

D T Pendit

THIS IS ME

This is me, who I am,
What I do and where I go.
How you see me, is how I'll be,
Now, today, and forever this way.
This woman's body, is my own,
From a little child, I have grown.
In middle age, I have got wise,
And not only see, with my eyes.
For of the world, I was blind,
But now in the Lord, I'm different you'll find.
For God will reveal the things I don't know,
Because He loves His people so.
Those who believe in God and His son,
The Lord will protect, until the world is done.

Amen.

Julia Smith

WHEN NIGHT IS COME

Darkness sliding quietly down the sky to cover all
Enfolds the sleeping millions like a soft war shawl
Young lovers made more perfect by the pale moon's golden light
Keep their tryst with none but starry chaperones in sight
When night is come

The green and sunlit places which invite a child to play
Two faced will harbour villains at the closing of the day
No happy laughter then, but muffled screams - a sudden thud
The hawthorn bushes red not just with berries but with blood
When night is come

In daylight hours what anguish hides behind a merry mask
While mind and body grapple with each mundane daily task
But when evening shadows deepen, strength and purpose fall apart
Like a dam whose walls have crumbled pain goes flooding through
the heart
When night is come.

A Wild

Magic

If wizard Merlin were alive today
He'd look around our wondrous world and say,
'It's magic.'

Airborne on metal wings I see men fly,
They gird the earth, non-stop, in orbit high,
That's magic.

Like shooting stars they reach the moon and back
Controlled by buttons on a console's rack.
Great magic.

And men converse across the ocean wide,
Their voices clear as if sat side by side.
Deep magic.

Then there is mystic satellite TV
Enchanted mirrors, what else could they be?
Sky magic.

But does satanic mischief lie in store?
Disease-filled armaments and total war!
Black magic.

Merlin fear not! for Good will conquer sin
Our Great Creator will not let evil win!
God's Magic.

Lydia Webster

DIED

Darkness falls
I think I collapsed
My girlfriend calls
In my eyes, my life does flash
Unable to move, I cannot breathe
What is this vague recollection of my past?
My girlfriend's on her knees
My eyes open slowly
The light brings pain
I can't feel the ground below me
I can't feel the rain
Her tears drop upon my cheek
Not here, not now
My body feels so weak
I cannot even think how
This situation came to be
I'm drifting away
Can this really be happening to me?
I hear her cry, begging me to stay
But the piercing in my head begins to subside
Princess, I can't stay here with you
Cos I've just died.

Craig Stewart

ECHOES

Echoes of silence resounded through depths of despair
wandering in time and space knowing he isn't there
silence that fills me was once just an echoing roar
silence engulfs me where once I could see eagles soar.

Echoes of silence consume all my night and my day
a cavernous void of despair keeps my anger at bay
silence inside me destroys all the sounds that I love
and a squawking magpie which mimics the sound of a dove.

Echoes of silence compound as I lay on my bed
as love turns to hate with all these tears I have shed
echoes of laughter receded as silence invades
the dream is for real as reality silently fades.

Echoes of silence resounded through depths of despair
the sound of his voice which beckoned me into his lair
silence still fills me with sorrow and turbulent roar
my life is now nothing; once I could see eagles soar.

Judy Studd

CARRIE

The day you were born I'll never forget
The love between us was already set
The look on my face must have said it all
We'd rushed to the hospital after getting the call

You opened your eyes and looked at me
The love I felt was plain to see
You had downy hair and eyes of brown
And on your face you wore a funny little frown

Your mam was exhausted but clearly happy
And your dad, well he was worrying about changing your nappy
I was proud as proud can be
Because I'd just had my first grandchild given to me.

Gail Wooton

MOVING ON

Country walks and seaside talks,
Jupiter's position and my admission,

That it's still you and how that makes me blue.

Forever your memory tattooed on my heart,
No way for me to erase your part.

Days, months, years go by,
And still your haunting makes me cry.

Heaven sent, my soul's twin,
Still you never really let me in.

You held it all back, from even yourself,
I ask you now, who gets to share that wealth?

I hope you find someone, something, an outlet for your grief,
As for me, I have no self-belief,

You shattered me and didn't even watch to see
How I picked up the pieces to make a stronger me.

Yes, I guess I am stronger, though lonelier now,
But I will find someone, someday, somehow . . .

Thanks for showing me that I want that for my life,
Perhaps that lesson was worth the strife.

I know I can't go on blaming you forever,
I have to put myself right and it really is now or never.

No more missed opportunities, I've had enough of being scared,
I'm determined to believe that deep down you cared,

And that it's possible to be cared for again,
Indeed there's a whole world of men.

Many more are just like you, I'm sure,
But hundreds, thousands, with hearts so pure.

I've recently found one, who likes me a lot,
And when I was with him, I almost completely forgot
You.

Alexa Crawford

A LONE STAR

Lying down, alone and sad
Thinking of the memories I once had
Some of them bring a smile to my face
Some of them take my love with haste
Tears of joy and smiles of sadness
Thinking of you fills my head with madness
For what you had done that day in the sun
When we were having so much fun
You left me there all by myself
Like a lone book on an empty shelf
I could read your face, without a trace
That you wished I would trip up, over my shoelace!

Getting up and walking around
Moving towards a beating sound
Not knowing it was my aching heart
Hurting me when we broke apart
Wishing we were together now
Makes me want to ask you, how?
How did this happen to you and me?
We etched our names on the bark of a tree
We walked hand in hand through the park
Whether it was light or pitch-dark
I remember the day we first kissed
I forgot to tell you there is something I missed
This never happened, it's only a wish.

Garry Traynor

LIFE'S SHELL

I feel so empty
a total mess,
so full of despair
confusion, distress.
Can't think of a future
just ruled by the past,
My body unsure
how long it can last.
So tired and scared
living in Hell,
No one to talk to,
no one to tell.
No one understands
these feelings inside
They can't see the ones
I desperately hide.
So tired of the fighting
trying to live,
Struggling through life
with nothing left to give.

Kelly Morris

THE DAY THE WORLD FELL APART

Someone, just swallow me up whole
I want to be in a corner, curled up in a ball.
Help me 'cause I'm falling
With no bottom at all.

I'm reaching out for a hand
But all that is there
Is a long cold emptiness
And a blackness to despair.

Listen to me, I'm calling,
Friend, just lend me an ear
'Cause I'm still falling
With the drop of my tear.

Deeper and deeper, I fall into the depths
Can't see no way out.
Help me I'm falling
I scream and I shout.

I think of the worthless
Of my life that has become,
And think of ending
What can't be undone.

I plan to run away
As far as I can go
But this blackness still catches me
I'm just far too slow.

Somebody put answers to my questions
And please put me back on track
Someone love me for what I am
And give me back what I lack.

It's deep in the summer
But I'm as cold as the snow
As the storm clouds move in, it rains
But I've got nowhere to go.

Standing here, rain washes over me
And everything goes black.
It won't be long now
As death touches my back.

June the 18th 2004
Another day in history.

Stuart Adams

TAKEN FOR GRANTED

Everything we own
Even our home
Is taken for granted
Even plants planted
We should love our world
Love every boy and girl
Our television sets
Or the things we get
We don't do enough
We should help with stuff
In the great outdoors
We should have clean floors
But we think there are people
Who'll do it for us
But they won't, so
We'll have to take the bus

Megan Jay Paul (10)

BEATING THE BULLIES

When I started school
I thought it would be great
I never knew that it would be
The thing I would most hate

Waking in the morning
Knowing what was ahead
Wishing it was the weekend
So I could stay in bed

Making the dreaded journey
Through the entrance gate
My heart beating really fast
Feeling like someone's bait

Stepping into the classroom
The whispering would start
A group of friends laughing loud
Of which I wished I was a part

After High School I was stronger
And no longer did I fear
Those petty, immature bullies
That made me shed those tears

When I started college
I made school a thing of the past
I succeeded in my goals
And how college was a blast.

Natalie L West

GRATEFUL TO BE SOBER

Today I am grateful
To be sober
I am standing up straight
Not constantly falling over

Gone are the bumps
And bruises on my head
My eyes are bright and clear
Not fireball-red

Gone is the desire
To drink like a fish
It's crystal clear when I talk
Not gobbledegook or gibberish

No arguments or violence anymore
The police aren't knocking
At my door
There's no more talk of
The nutter house or funny farm
With sobriety you see
I cause no one any harm

And now that I have had time
To stop and think
I realise I was powerless
Over the demon drink

I suffer from an illness
That will never be over
But today I am grateful
To be sober

G Quinney

THE COWARD

To call a man a coward
Is the worst thing of all
To confess so sincere
Is caused by such fear
And to be cursed, forever small.

Philip Allen

A NEW DAY

As dawn breaks through the midnight sky,
a figure looks down with a watchful eye,
soaring through the moon, stars and sun,
guiding and protecting each special loved one.

No longer having a body or mind,
to give kisses, hugs and words of kind,
no more dreaming of the days yet to come,
or talking for hours with that special someone.

There's no feeling the cool breeze through your hair,
no more opening your heart and being laid bare,
no more tears, pain, laughter or fun,
or feeling of warmth on your face from the sun.

Here it's calm, quiet, a place filled with love,
looking down from the clouds, from far up above,
away from everyone and being apart
watching so closely, those in your heart.

As dawn breaks through the midnight sky,
a figure looks down with a watchful eye,
soaring through the moon, stars and sun,
guiding and protecting each special loved one.

Louisa Dean

HAVE NO REGRETS

Let's all forget about our bad past,
Live life to the full and have a blast,
You could be anything that you want to be,
Live life to the full, be young and free.
Just remember along the way,
To be a good person you don't have to pray,
If you are gentle and you are kind
More people will like you
I think you'll find.
When you look back upon your past,
Have no regrets because life can go fast.
When you think of the bad times
It does you no good,
You start to feel sad and misunderstood.
Try not to argue, try not to fight,
Try to do well and you'll be so bright.
Never forget the golden rule
Live life for today -
Don't be a fool.

Joanne Owen

THE TEA PARTY

'Please do come and take tea with me.'
A sweet old lady made her plea.
Far too long she'd been alone
By a silent telephone.

'So sorry but I'm busy now.
I'll come and see you soon, somehow.
I must go now; I'm very late,
Rushing for a luncheon date.'

The lady walked on for a while,
Her face wearing a tired smile;
Then she raised her hand to greet
Someone from across the street.

'I've not seen you for such a time;
I'm pleased you're looking really fine.'
Before she could make her reply,
Her neighbour said, 'Well, I must fly.'

'Please do come and take tea with me.'
A sweet old lady made her plea.
For too long she'd been alone
By a silent telephone.

Hazel Mills

MY LITTLE ANGEL SLEEP

Sweet little angel just close your eyes,
Travel you will to a different time,
Where the sun shines long and laughter's heard,
As you will be in a new place on Earth.
Love will surround you in many forms
You'll be so well and feel so warm.

You will play with angels in a beautiful place
Where all is gentle you'll feel so safe,
See you're an angel sent from above
For you my dearest, I have such love,
You're all my hopes and dreams come true
Remember my angel, I'm always with you.

Past dearest loved ones you will see
In a beautiful world soon you will be,
When the morning comes your dream's complete,
They will send you back again to me
My dearest love, please do not weep
Rest your eyes and go to sleep.

Beverley Odle

A LINCOLNSHIRE VILLAGE CALLED NOCTON

Now when I was a young man and lived in Main Street
You knew everyone who lived there, whom you met in the street
There was the 'Ladymeet' dairy herd on the Manor Farm
They have now built eleven houses there, very little charm

You could go out at night without locking the door
There would be a 'Bobby' about on his bike, that's for sure
The kids could go round the village, anywhere they liked
And were equally as safe, riding round on their bikes.

The vicar Kenneth Healey lived next to the graveyard
He was always there, helping with any question too hard
Mr Eminson the Headmaster, was always about
He lived in the School House, he was always there,
Just give him a shout

The traffic was just average and we had the hospital near
But we never seemed to worry, we had nothing to fear
There was never a problem when men were working nearby
The kids could go in the fields, they would ask the men working
What they were doing and why?

There wasn't much money to be earned at the time
But we seemed to be able to pay our bills just in time
There was no money for smoking, drinking beer or gadding about
The aim was to keep the bailiffs away, you never heard of a lager lout

But Santa brought presents at Christmas to all little girls and boys
And you would get an apple, an orange, some sweets,
Nuts and small toys
We had fetés on the lawn around the beautiful Nocton Hall
The Commander at the hospital would open them, just give him a call

The Sunday Schools were thriving at Nocton and Wasp Nest
                                                    Social Hall
The Reverend Kenneth Healy would be there helping -
Always there at your call
We had an organised bus trip to the seaside every year
When most of the families on the day, would be there

Len Woodhead

DREAMING

Sweet thoughts in a dream
Dreaming of towns where I go
The streets are dumb with snow
Thick fog came creeping down
Like a bubble over the town
No one at all in sight
As we hurry through the night
Deep silence where shadows cease
Everything is quiet, everything at peace.

Ann Thompson

USELESS TEARS

I wish my tears could help,
but I know they can't.
She's human just like me,
but now she can't see.

She was just a young girl,
so much she could have seen.
She never fired a gun;
she just wanted to have fun.

A bullet in her classroom
and suddenly it's gone.
A casualty of war,
a bloody disgrace for sure.

A postcard from a war zone
where men with honour show none.
The mother's tears will stay;
could you keep that hate at bay?

Over there in the Gaza strip
a child's life is destroyed,
and will the gunman say sorry?
An army without glory.

There will be more like her,
more tragedies in God's eyes.
They're still paying the price;
as peace is kept on ice.

Anthony Welsh

GROWING OLD, UNGRACIOUSLY

At what age do you feel old?
Fifty! Sixty! Or beyond that?
Do your bones ache without reason?
Mine do and that's a fact.

The doctor helps when he can
With tablets to stop the achin'.
Alas they seem to have little effect
So eventually they're forsaken.

Each day is harder than before
'Cause you want to stay in bed.
The mind is willing, the body is not
There's no more to be said.

Acupuncture and reflexology
Herbal tea, Ginseng and stuff,
You've tried all these alternatives
But when is enough, enough?

The eyesight has worsened
Your hearing's not the same,
You cannot comprehend the reason
Is it just old age to blame?

Your memory slowly fades
It becomes harder to recall,
The things you should be doing
If doing anything at all.

Your old age is coming fast
Faster than you may think,
The aches, the pains, the dementia
Would turn anyone to drink.

George S Johnstone

PRECIOUS BEAUTY

Precious beauty, asleep in my arms,
My total love will keep you from harm,
Dreaming of days when the sun always shines,
You're always there, right on my mind.

Right on my mind, you're always there,
Others may try but they do not compare,
Looking at you my heart always sings,
For you arrived on angels' wings.

On angels' wings you arrived,
To break through the cobwebs of deceit and lies,
To show the world how to delve deep inside,
As God's messenger, precious and kind.

Precious and kind, God's messenger you are,
You radiate love as bright as a star,
Healing all wounds past and present,
The Masters support you from the moon's crescent.

From the crescent moon, the Master's view,
To help and encourage you in all that you do.
To keep you strong, determined and whole,
They are right with you to achieve your goal.

To achieve your goals they're always there,
To end all suffering and ease all despair.
No longer dreaming, as the sun shines each day,
Precious beauty, your vibrancy sparkles and guides the way.

Sara Church

YORKSHIRE LIFE

The bleak wind blows across the hill,
He sits in the corner, feels the chill,
The weatherman has forecast gales,
Coming across those Yorkshire Dales.
He sees the first few flakes of snow,
To get his sheep in, he must go,
He calls out for his dog to come to hand,
And heads out into the rugged land.
Clambering the rough old track,
To bring his sheep safely back,
Back in the yard now are the sheep,
This is life on the Yorkshire moors,
But it is the land this man adores.

Michael Scott

GOT NO TIME

My hubby loves golf and he does it very well
Whether he enjoys every game, it is hard to tell

Practising in the hallway from morning 'til night
Pretends he has a golf club, swings it left to right

I think every day he would love to tee off at nine
But he goes to a place called work and doesn't have any time.

Barbara Jackson

Millie 'B'

Welcome to Millie 'B'
The newest member of our family,
So much like your sister Luci Lou,
No wonder we are in love with you.
You are so beautiful, little one,
I hope your life will be full of fun,
And Beatrice being your middle name
Means our initials are the same.
My nan, my mum and me
And now of course you, Millie 'B'.

We are so lucky you are alive,
You really battled to survive.
You will be another battling Beattie
I am sure -
Who could ask for anything more?
Sleeping so peacefully, so content,
Millie 'B' you have been heaven sent.

Maureen Arnold

FAIRGROUND FUN

Shouts of laughter
Screams of joy
Boy with girl
Girl with boy
Parents with children
Holding hands tight
One bang in the sky
Causes fright and delight

The smell of hot dogs
Wafting through the air
Candyfloss and chips
Such a joy to share
Bumper cars, roller coasters, helter-skelter too
What next to go on?
Let's join a queue

We'll try the ghost train
See what it's like
Searching out things
That go 'bump' in the night
Hook a duck and see what we win
Cuddly toys or a bottle of gin!

The night is over all too soon
The only light left
Is that of the moon
So many adventures and fun to be had
Visiting the fairground
With Mom and Dad.

Ruth Fellows

WINGED WISDOM

I am king in the air
I am lord of my sky
Clouds whisper to me as I'm winging by
Hook, talon, beak, claw
And keen of the eye
There is death in my clutch, fear in my cry
I swiftly approach when my victim I spy
It's natural to me
You humans ask why
But we all have to do things to live or to die
The young in the eerie with crops to be filled
For me it's ordained
A purpose fulfilled
But what is your purpose
I watch from above
With actions so devious not fashioned by love
Such behaviour for humans I hardly approve
But I'm only the eagle God intended to be
Not created like you to create posterity

Ron Powell

UNTITLED

She was so very small
No one saw her at all
From the corner of the eye
A leaf, wind blown by -

A little Jenny wren
Lived in my hedge, and then
The Council came, my hedge they stole
Leaving poor Jenny in the cold.

The hedge I've planted back
And I've left food for her there,
But I don't see the little wren
And I've looked everywhere . . .

Jacqueline Taylor

CATHERINE WHEELS

To start the show, a Catherine wheel
Whizzing through the night.
Its sparks all spinning round and round
In gold and silver light.

It spins and spins through the night,
Its circle begins so slow.
But round and round and round and round
Ever faster, it will go.

Catherine wheels so deadly bright,
Round it sparks will spray
'Don't stand too close, it's very hot!'
The officers all say.

It slows right down, comes to a halt
The sparks no longer fly.
The show is over - say goodnight,
Farewell and goodbye.

Beth Harrison

THE KISS OF LIFE . . .

That first tender kiss on newborn baby's brow,
Brings the whole meaning of life together somehow.

That first awkward kiss, when you go to school,
When you stand in a crowd and feel a fool.

The first sloppy kiss from a favourite aunt,
It leaves you breathless and makes you pant.

The first meaningful kiss on your first date,
And you think you've found someone,
To be your soul-mate.

That first passionate kiss when you're in your teens,
Emotions get strong and affects your genes.

That eternal kiss when you meet at the altar
And you believe everything's rosy and will never falter.

That endearing kiss that comes with the band of gold
And lasts a lifetime as you both grow old.

That final kiss as you lie on your bed,
Life's passed you by . . .
Now you're dead.

Roy Perkins

COLOUR BLIND

Black was black and white was white
we were told when we were young,
Never mix the two together, was the song
so loudly sung.
We never played with children
unless their skin was white,
Somehow we all seemed to know
it just would not be right.
So we grew up not knowing
coloured people or their culture,
But it did not seem wrong to us
only second nature.

Then one day skin colours
stopped influencing me,
They had all blended together
so that I could not see
The difference between the colours
brown, yellow, black or white,
And now I know that in my youth
it simply wasn't right,
To let the prejudices of others
affect and spoil my view,
Of others who looked different
because they were human too.

I'm sure the world we live in
would be a far better place,
If we'd learnt as children
not to segregate by race,
No one showed us by example
what was good or what was mean,
Now we know the lessons taught
really should have been,
Look behind the face
and see what lies within,
Don't simply judge a person
by the colour of their skin.

Beverley Balogh

FOOTBALL FEVER

Football, football, give me a break
England lost, they're having a wake
David Beckham, Wayne Rooney and the rest
Played their hearts out and did their best
But it wasn't enough, they got beat
Greece came up trumps, with passing so neat
Never mind the World Cup is now our aim
Shouldn't forget - it's only a game!

Shirley Jaggard

ALONE

Like a king on a throne,
Wind blown,
Unknown,
Without a groan,
Or even a moan.
The birds have flown,
I am thrown
Into a comfort zone,
Resting prone.
Without a phone,
No ringing tone,
Not even aircraft drone,
No one to turn a stone.
Happily, alone!

Robert Collins

KEEPING HIM ALIVE

The nurse said, 'He's in good hands.
Time you went on with your life.'
She acted as if he was already dead,
Not caring that I was his wife.

I've taken good care of the one I love
As his life now begins to grow dim.
He's been part of my life for so long,
I don't *want* to be rid of him.

She said, 'It is as if he's died
But you can't bury the body . . .'
I was stunned by her lack of compassion.
That shouldn't be said to anybody.

How cold can one person be?
But then, she doesn't love him the way I do.
She never thought before she spoke,
I brought to an end that interview.

He's like a five-year-old with autism,
And delights in breaking things.
But when the music starts to play,
He lifts up his head and sings.

I won't let them put him away,
I'll carry on for as long as I can.
I was always his 'old lady'
He'll always remain my 'old man'.

Polly Davies

NO PLAY

Don't you dare go out to play
There's danger lurking everywhere
Don't try handstands or climb trees
You might take a nasty tumble
And graze those childish knees.

Playing around with a yo-yo
Is certainly a no go
Skipping ropes are definitely out,
You may give someone a nasty clout.

For goodness sake, don't try to fly
There'd be an ambulance on stand-by
Hopscotch, you could trip and break a toe
And for heaven's sake, don't brandish a toy gun
Or off to the slammer you will go.

Playing a game of tag can make you breathless
Riding a bike, oh no, it's far too reckless
Making daisy chains was considered very tame
But even that is out of bounds
As Boffins say, they spread germs around.

Children of yesteryear, when they took a tumble
Picked themselves up and washed their scabby
Knees without a grumble
Now the list of don'ts is endless
But the freedom to run and play
Has been eroded away.

If children are denied the freedom to play outside
Best they stay in a rocking chair inside
Or perhaps they can spend the time
Knocking spots off each other
While listening to their yelling mother.

Rachel McKie

GROWING WITH GREENS

Kylie the caterpillar
ate and ate and ate.
She always had seconds
heaped upon her plate.

'Greens are very good for me.
It was my mother's belief.'
So laughing, she sat down to dine
and ate another leaf.

Then one day it was time to stop
and spin a silky thread.
Said Kylie with a happy smile,
'Goodnight, it's time for bed.'

Now elegance is to the fore
a butterfly is Kylie,
with tiny waist and painted wings.
All things we praise most highly.

Jillian Merer

THE BALLAD OF SHOOTER'S HILL

We're weeping for our Willie, our erstwhile sheriff's shot,
There never was a braver man to die.
A fearless, lawless lawman, who'll never be forgot,
By whoso'er may mourn him, by and by.

Truth, fallacy or folklore, he stands above the crowd,
A gentle man's betrothal to his creed.
Not at all loquacious, nor even over-loud,
He spurned the very thought that bade him speed.

He'd amble in his gaiters and shuffle in his spurs,
And liquor-heads were open in his sway.
With bar-stools falling over, as each gun-hand itching stirs,
Whence dying in a huddle where they lay.

A legend in his lifetime, regaled by many still,
The coming of his passing - a surprise.
He single-handed slew them a-top of Shooter's Hill,
Tho' fatally, whilst cursing in his cries.

We carried him so slowly, his guns still in his hands,
With friend and foe forlornly side by side.
He eyed them in his dying, all rogues of many bands,
Then shot a grinning greenhorn ere he died.

He was a mean avenger, imbued with stoic charm,
Whose cold eye smote the sinner at a glance.
His mawkish, clueless manner, belied a sleepless arm,
And no one ever gained a second chance.

On Shooter's Hill he rests now, his plaque shines in the sun,
Among the many sheriffs, row on row.
His whittled name emboldened, our 'Willie-Don-A-Gun',
A bullet hole, his epitaph below.

Derek Haskett-Jones

BEWITCHED, BUGGYD AND BEWILDERED

Head down, concentrate
Try to miss the garden gate

Use the road, it's easier there
Even though the drivers glare

Excuse me dear, try not to fret
I'm just not used to steering yet

Accelerate but not too much
It only needs a gentle touch

Turn the corner on two wheels
Now I know how Jenson feels

Look out Sir! I'm coming through
Well I *did* get there ahead of you

No, don't ask me to reverse
Oh how rude! No need to curse

Now where's the brake, how do I stop?
I want to go into that shop

Shut my eyes and cross the road
Oops! That lorry's lost its load

I hope he isn't blaming me
I'm big enough for him to see

Now let's not fall out over that
Just take me home - the battery's flat!

Betty Nevell

CALAMITY

Went to Spain, place Lacarla.
Hubbie's died, travelling farther.
Airport, experiencing hustle and bustle,
It's my age, I get in a tussle.
Customs, I set off the alarm,
Attendant quickly held my arm,
Frisked, felt everso queer,
Keys, a voice said, 'Okay my dear,'
Alighted the plane with my kith and kin,
In a hustle, void of a din,
A baby started to cry,
'Tilly's fallen asleep,' her mother said, with a sigh.
Grandaughter's ears started to pop,
A sign the plane had set off.
Bag and baggage, we'd reached the apartment,
They'd had a fire, I start to relent,
Ground floor apartment assumed we'd booked,
Lost my tongue, I simply looked.
Transferred to the first floor,
Relieved we had a key to the door.
I settled for a cup of tea,
Weary, oh woe is me!
Daughter adamant to settle the matter,
Early morning workmen causing a clatter.
Glanced at this terrible sight,
Chipping plaster with all their might.
Stood out a mile an electrical fault,
Daughter made a necessary complaint.
No fire alarm, no extinguishers, imagination - I feel faint
Had the audacity to uplift the bill,
The lift had come to a standstill.
Managed to get a refund
Now an apartment, back of beyond.
Thank God the holiday had ended,
To England we now descended.

Alice Harrison

THE EXCITEMENT OF YOUTH

Swirling and twirling, the excitement of life,
Dancing and prancing with feelings of delight,
The music, the power under dazzling lights
Bodies tremble as feelings rise to great heights.

The force of such energy all through the night,
Defeat unthinkable until day sheds its light.
Exhausted figures, so unusual to see
They wilt and crumble without dignity.

Water passed quickly from one to another,
Revival at last, soon to recover,
There's no slowing down, no time to be lost
As caution to the wind now willingly tossed.

Persistent music throbbing, pounding in ears
Going faster and faster, youth has no fears
With the swirling and twirling continuing on
As if excitement of life has just begun.

Dawn now breaking, haunting music goes on
With daylight soon appearing excitement now gone
From a scene, exhausting, as tiring can be,
Satisfaction, contentment, plainly to see.

Sleep of revival, replenishment of youth,
To awake, unwelcome, stark moment of truth
As half-open eyes squint with pain from bright light
Recovery impossible from effects of that night.

But youth is so powerful, all systems in place,
Recovery behind them take on another race,
Excitement ever-growing, where's the next show?
They're dressed for the occasion again in full flow.

So soon all the wonder of youth then fleets by
Sadly gone, the excitement, we'll never know why.

Irene Grahame

THE RED BALL

I once had a ball - a shiny red ball
Given to me as I started to crawl.
It bounced and it rolled and crept out of view
So that I couldn't find it and screamed - wouldn't you?

As I got bigger I learned how it bounced
And managed to catch it when on it I pounced.

When I started school I played catch-if-you-can
With friends in the playground chasing it as it ran.

I still had it in junior school, rosy and red
And we threw it against the old bicycle shed.

At senior school basketball was the *in thing*
I practised 'til I was crowned *Basketball King*.

When I left school I frequented the park
Throwing ball after ball at the net until dark.

The local scout saw me and took me in hand
And I played for my County, a feat I had planned.

Success I'd achieved and now could walk tall
But I couldn't have done it without my red ball.
Was this a dream? I'll leave you to guess,
Maybe it's *no* but then maybe it's *yes!*

Paddy Jupp

OF COURSE!

Of course I'm over him now
Don't worry, it's passed,
Really wanted this to work
The glow didn't last.
Initial excitement gave way to deep pain
Expectations defeated again and again,
It should have been alright,
The years we had known each other -
I wanted commitment, a steady partner,
A caring lover!
He wanted to be a brother, a mate, a friend at his convenience.
He had no time for me,
That's it then, it had to end.
We could have made a difference
It made everything worse,
Got on with life, what must be, must be -
Except in my unguarded golden dreams, of course.

Sue Woodbine

HERE'S TO ELIZABETH

So gallant a girl, not long a bride,
Stricken with grief for the father who'd died,
Stepped down from a plane one sad noontide
To take up the reins of her duty.

Not for her now, any private life;
Limited times to be mother and wife;
It's the public pageantry, drum and fife,
That mark out the terms of her duty.

A lifetime of service none could deny,
As the years have fled and the world's gone awry.
Now the media harass and tabloids stand by
Hoping she'll fail in her duty.

Greedy, her people, with envious eyes
Complain about privilege but can't surmise
The weight of the burden. Still, they'd criticise
If she took a break from her duty.

So gallant a lady, past seventy, still
She toils in our service and works with a will.
When we'd have retired long since she'll fulfil
The relentless requirements of duty.

So here's to Elizabeth! Long may she reign!
We are grateful for freedoms she's helped to sustain
And we'll shout hurrah, again and again
As we watch her performing her duty.

Anne Wild

NOVEMBER DELIGHT

Coat buttoned up
Woolly scarf pulled tight
Five . . . Four . . . Three
Two . . . One . . . ignite!
With a piercing whistle
Rocket shoots into the night
Then the boom and bang
Bring hollers of delight.
The burst of colours
That explode for show
Yellows, greens and reds
Flutter like coloured flakes of snow.
As they dissolve into the darkness
We revel in pyrotechnic afterglow
Whoosh . . . there goes another one
Stand back and watch it go.

Keith Tissington

REALITY

As quick as a wink, when you blink it's gone,
And our memories are jogged by the lines of a song.
'Tis more precious than a nugget of gold,
The opposite we fear, there's no one as bold.

We take it for granted as we wake in the morn,
Never give it a thought as the day starts to dawn.
Happy Birthday! Good Luck! We all wish you well,
What tomorrow will bring, only the good Lord can tell.

Money, possessions, what good is all that,
If when you're old, on your own you are sat?
Be grateful, obliging, just cope with the strife,
'Cause you have it all, 'tis a gift that's called 'life'.

Jan Kelly

DECISIONS

I could have sent you roses
But they don't last long

I could have sent a record
For you to sing along

I could have sent you ribbons
To keep your hair in place

I could have sent you make-up
To put upon your face

I could have sent a letter
For you to read in bed

But I couldn't make my mind up
So I sent this poem instead.

Ken Mulligan

INSIDE A CAVE

Inside a cave, life has gone.
Inside a cave the sun has never shone.
Inside a cave is where I dread,
Inside a cave people are dead.
Inside a cave bones are found,
Inside a cave there is no sound.
Inside a cave I must not go,
Inside a cave is a definite *no!*

Alex Simm (9)

JUST YESTERDAY

Once I could run and jump and dance
My life was full of fun and romance
I chased the girls and caught a few
Yes, once I was young and fit like you

The city lights would beckon me
I'd be out all night 'til two or three
Burning the candle at both ends
Wining and dining with my friends

But now old age has slowed me down
I seldom venture into town
I'm not too steady on my feet
And I need time to cross the street

So spare a thought, if I pass your way
For though I may seem old and grey
That bright young spark that you are now
Was me, just yesterday!

Moira Yarwood

IF WAR MEMORIALS COULD TALK

If the war memorials could talk
What would the servicemen say
About the way that Britain is heading
In this new century, in the present day?

Tom a soldier up in the top corner
Calls out to Joe, an airman on the far right.
'What did we die for mate,
Why the heck did we bother to fight?'

'We died to save our country,' said Joe,
'To be free and not ruled by others.
To make our own decisions in government
For this we gave our lives and left our mothers!'

'Yes, that's what we thought,' said Tom,
'If the future we could have foreseen.
That Britain would join a Common Market,
With a hidden agenda, which wasn't seen.'

'You're right there Tom,' said Fred a sailor on the bottom row,
'Now they want us to give up the pound.
You know what they're heading for Joe?
To be ruled from a Parliament on foreign ground.'

You died on the Somme, deep in mud and blood
A Federal Union will be created with Great Britain a State,
The French and Germans will have won the battles
Because it was handed to them on a plate.

To the Toms, Joes, Freds and Johns who gave their lives for us
For they shalt not grow old!

David G Forsbrook

TORN

Problems are burying me, thick and fast,
I thought it would be alright, I knew it wouldn't last.

Cried so hard, can't cry anymore,
Tired, exhausted, my eyes are so sore.

Being tortured and tormented by a weakness you've found,
My world's been shattered, been turned upside down.

I hear the shouts and the blames,
Everything I'm used to has gone up in flames.

Once was solid as a rock, we stick together through thick and thin,
Was once as a unit, no one could get in.

We love each other and really care,
Someone would knock us, no one would dare.

You'd hurt the one and you'd get us all,
Kick one of us and we'd all fall.

Hearing others cry that hurts the most,
You see everyone happy, look at them boast.

If I'm unhappy, you should be too,
Why did this happen to me and not you?

Looking at me,
'Well what are you looking at?'
Asking, 'Are you alright?'
'I'm fine!' I spat.

'Well are you okay. Are you alright?'
I won't sit and cry. I won't go down without a fight.

You have to be the strong one and pull everyone through,
I can't do this alone, I'm human like you.

Friends coming up to me saying, 'I've been through it too.'
Well you don't know how I feel.
It's different for each and everyone of you.

You don't know how I feel, you can't comprehend,
It feels so different, it feels like the end.

Please don't leave me, I need you all,
We're weak as individuals but strong as a whole.

Everything's different, start new, start afresh,
Maybe I don't want that . . . well couldn't you have guessed?

Melanie May

LONELINESS

It's cloudy and dull with no sun in the sky,
Even the birds are forgetting to fly.
I look from my window but what do I spy?
Only my wash hanging limply to dry.

There's nothing to look at and nothing to see,
No one about to invite round for tea.
Has all of the world gone away to the sea?
Does everyone love a Bank Holiday but me?

Jacquie Russell

A VAST EMPTY SPACE

You kissed me and my heart soared
And I felt for a time
That all the treasures in this world
Would be forever mine.
There was a kind of magic
That touched my very soul.
I don't think you quite realised
How much I wanted more.
You turned and walked away from me,
Threw my love back in my face.
Now all that's left is loneliness
And a vast, empty space.

Rosemary Thomson

BOOKS

Books, collections of thoughts from so many,
Companions of quiet and peaceful hours,
Fountains of knowledge from a few pennies,
To priceless tomes in British Library towers.
Thousands of words lie between each cover,
Talking of people, places, events.
Take one off a shelf and you discover
You're in a different world which man invents.
In fiction, the imagination rides,
Characters growing, acting out their scenes.
In factual books, truth rules, nothing should hide
All the information 'Is' or 'Has been'.
What a wealth of living there is in books,
So many worthy of a second look!

Pat Heppel

THE DYING OF BOROMIR

A swift first arrow hit his arm,
The next pierced through his side,
Death's sting arrow hit his heart,
Searing pain he could not hide.
His new found friend knelt beside him,
He clasped both hands with fear,
'You fought with heart and honour.'
He held his friend with tears.
'I almost stole the ring,' he cried,
'My heart turned black to hold the power,
My true reward is now my death,
It stings to be my final hour.'
Aragorn moved closer to his whisper,
His face and eyes looked down with pity,
'You saved the bearer for your own death,
Now you will see your home . . . White City.'
With his last breath Boromir sighed,
'Will my people write a sonnet and sing,
Have I served with honour, just and right,
For my people, country and my king?'
Aragorn laid him softly to the Earth,
And wept with dismay and sorrow.
Gimli and Legolas knelt and vowed to him,
'We will avenge your death tomorrow!'

J Neville

THE GIRL IN THE LITTLE BLACK DRESS
WITH MYSTERIOUS DARK BROWN EYES
(She had that femme fatale way to hypnotise)

I met you in a city centre club, I really fancied you, I guess
you knew I would!
With your long raven hair and dark brown eyes, you had the
power to hypnotize!
You were wearing the ultimate little black dress;
There was something special about you, and this wasn't just a guess.
With a silver chain around your tantalising neck, so sweet and stunning
Even though I knew you had that extra special savoire faire,
I never knew what was coming.
With elegantly ample breasts glowing in low cut top and bare midriff
showing, and belly button too; I knew you were a young trend-setter
for your sweet navel was bravely pierced to add to your exquisite
daring view.
Here I just caught a glimpse of a delicate tattoo of a green serpent
below your delectable belly button, divine!
Like an extra dimension to hedonistic charm in a rhyme of beauty for
our time.

When you were dancing and raving around I saw you were also
wearing the latest sweetly baring bum-teaser string thong;
Proud of your young,well-rounded wiggling beauty as exquisitely
lovely as a well sung song.
I didn't realise then you were only eighteen, I put you in the middle
twenties and enjoying your own enchanting scene.
By then I'd already caught your mysterious brown eyes with hidden
depths glowing; And engaged you in small talk and your sweet lips
parted with merry laughter cascading in all you were showing.
Soon we were dancing closely together on the floor with passions rising
and bodies swaying;
By then words didn't matter for I knew you were speaking with
what your hips were saying.
In a shady alcove of the club we soon were enjoying torrid French
kisses and feverish intimate caresses too.
As only complete love hungry strangers are able so to do.

I was amazed when you invited me back to your trendy little flat;
And soon we completed what love at first sight started and I was very
pleased with that.
And although now you are my regular extra special teenage date;
I will always remember our first meeting which must have been fate.
I'm over forty and you are a radiantly sweet eighteen
year old girl;
And your little black dress and the way you wore same with flair,
will always remind me of our first kiss and your sweet teasing
romantic twirl.

Johnnie J Docherty

LIFE IS TOO SHORT

Life is too short
or so they say.
If this is so,
why let is slip away?
'Do we have to do that?'
'I've not got the time.'
'I'll look at it later.'
'I'm sure it'll be fine.'
These precious little minutes
tick-tocking past,
they don't spare a thought
they're gone in a flash.
We sit there complaining
with nothing to do.
Bored!
In this world?
What's wrong with you?
Open your eyes wide like the sun.
Grasp each moment
get every little thing done.
Take nothing for granted
don't just walk on by.
Tell someone you love them
you don't know when it's goodbye.
Breathe deeply, then deeper
feel the air in your lungs.
Play like a child
sing songs you'd once sung.
Let your soul be full of
ambitions and dreams.
'Carpe diem!'
(whatever that means!)

Take hold of your life
use it as you will.
It's a very special gift
which is only yours to fill.
I hope when I'm old, well
a high number and a nought
I'll sit down and say,
'Isn't life too short?'

Sophie Nicolaysen

JUST ONE

Where and when did they all go?
Given me - near fifty years ago -
Bought in a beautiful china shop
Perfect and pretty - gold round the top.

Flowers so delicate painted all around -
Stored for so long while we travelled round -
Singapore, Germany, Cyprus, Hong Kong,
Malaysia, Holland, we moved with the crowd.

Coming out of the packing it seemed to say
Don't put me away for another day!
So we loved and used the china fine
Elegantly for years we all dined.

Can't think when and how, they dwindled away
Children washing up! But they had a long day:
Memories now are held by one piece,
A cream jug, with love ever always to keep.

I wouldn't have it different
The pleasure we shared -
Family round the table - we loved and cared
Now when the special piece comes with the cream
Oh look - they say - 'Do you remember our meals?'

What times we all had, seems long ago now,
Dad at the head, me at the bow -
The laughter and jokes as we had the meal,
Now! There's just me and a cream jug to fill.

P Morrill

APPEAL

Please, do not fell that tree.
I feel the blade will cut through me.
Come, look upon this grand old man,
Refrain from murder if you can.

Reflect on what his forebears meant
To human fast development.
Bows and arrows sailing ships
Barques of oak and launching slips.
Plainsmans shelters strong and sound.
Tables square and tables round.
Trees with shade from scorching sun,
Trees with fruits for everyone.

Pause my friend and stay your saw,
Reflect upon these things with awe.

C Joyce

AFTER THE FLOOD

Now fields and woods are green again,
and bluebells scent the air.
It's hard to recall those dark wet days
that filled us with despair.

The wind and driving icy rain
that just would not subside.
Stranded sheep and cattle,
and sadly many died.

Now storms are passed and life goes on,
with content for all creation.
For all the hardships we endured,
there is always compensation!

Seasons come and seasons go,
leaving memories good and bad.
Time is the biggest healer
to those who still feel sad.

Look around and you will see
that nature is so fair.
Forget those awful dreary days
when spring is in the air!

Greta Gaskin

THE TYRANT

I fled the library, for all the books
Were bound and written by the Tyrant's hand;
I dashed through streets, yet every face and look
Bore traces of the Tyrant's cold command.
I found an old, murky church and tried to pray,
But he had replaced the preacher there;
I found a lively market and tried to stay,
But the stalls would only sell his wares.
At last, with weary legs, and feet grown sore,
I hastened back toward my home for rest:
Drawing the curtains - bolting every door,
I refused all news, and received no guest.
    Yet there is nowhere, nowhere at all, to hide:
    The Tyrant has my life - he lives inside.

Matthew Graham Scarsbrook

POPPIES

More than ever I've seen them this year,
Somehow it seems so right,
By roadsides, in ditches, on roundabouts,
Their colour shining bright.

Shining like a beacon of hope,
With troubled times still here,
Wherever you go,
Their presence will show
A message of hope so clear.

A breeze picks up, the poppies stir,
And nod their heads as though -
With this year marking sixty summers
since D-Day -
They seem to know . . .

Stuart Powell

TODAY'S LESSON

Terror filled eyes staring through blood splattered faces,
Gun fire, explosions, from different places,
Choking smoke, confusion and stifled cries,
Is this the moment when humanity dies?
Yet this is not the front line from World War One,
Only a school where children are taught, learn, and have fun!

T J Dean

POSTED TO THE DECCAN

'Is this the Land of the wondrous East I came so far to see?
Is this the Land of silk and gold - the land of the Mystic Three?'
'Yes, this is the Land you came to see - desert sand your gold;
Your silk is but a spider's web - forgotten, shrivelled, old.'

'Where are all the rich green vales they said were quite close by?'
'They're the long crude ox-ploughed rows, coffins for maize and rye.'
'But what of the marbled silver courts they built in times of old?'
'Oh, they're the jagged soulless rocks - sinister, black and cold.'

'When shall I see the beautiful girls they hinted I would find?'
'They're just dreams that come by night to thwart the tortured mind'
'What of the sapphires, rubies and jade said to be plenteous here?'
'Oh, they're the stones, the fossiled crabs and hooves of vultured deer.'

'What of the flowing embroidered robes they said that I would wear?'
'Oh, they're the monsoon creeper shoots, plaited and
                                          woven with care.'
'Where are all the humming birds they told me hovered here?'
'Oh, they're the sari'd carrier girls that stop their work to stare.'

'Elephants, too, they said there'd be - llamas and beautiful birds?'
'No, just scorpions to sting you; white ants to eat you; lizards
who freeze on the wall - plus snakes and creatures that crawl.'

'The palms, the beaches, the starlit sky - tell me where are they?'
'Oh, beyond the scrub and the windswept plain that stretches far away.'

'Is there nothing, then, of what I was told that I was sure to see?'
'You must wait, young man, till you've done your time - and earned a
                                          reward maybe,
for this is the Land of the Deccan Plain,
the Land where the cactus grows -
this is the Land where you're destined to live -
the Land that nobody knows.'

Edward Fursdon

A MASSAGE

When I have my massage . . .
I've no real demands.
My feet and toes, they look OK
And oh, I like my hands.
If you could kindly focus
On the bits that fall between.
I'd not have to try so hard
To keep them all unseen.
Just realign my wonky spine
And make me one inch taller.
And while you're on my waistline
Please, I'd like it a bit smaller.
There's storage space, in my face
So, empty the bags by my eyes.
And my real wish, is if you could squish
The latte froth out of my thighs!

Vivienne C Wiggins

THE CALL OF THE DRUM - A LAUNCHING OF THE 'ZETLAND' AT REDCAR IN 1803

Nature's forces are in conflict tonight
Raging storm, thunder claps, lightning's blinding light
Faintly a tap, tap, tapping supersedes nature's might

'Tis the insistent call of the snare drum
Tum ti tum, titi tum, tum ti tum
Tum ti tum, titi tum, tum ti tun

Come Along, Bonnie Lads, Come Along
We need you Bonnie Lads, Come Along
To bend an oar Bonnie Lads, Come Along

Bobbing lanterns reflecting in bull's eye windowpane
Like fireflies dancing down Smithie's Lane
Glinting on the cobbles saturated with rain
Doors slamming, excitement mounting, running feet
Boots pounding down narrow winding cobbled street
Responding to the snare drummer's urgent beat

'Five for the White, Five on the Blue,
Four on red, Five to complete the Crew
Come on Bonnie Lads, We're relying on You.'

Launching crew rush her down the beach
Thro' the surf, float her out of reach
Of crashing waves, Dipping oars pull to the 'Mary Leach'

Eighty years 'Zetland' answered the Call of the 'Drum!'
Five hundred souls saved was her total sum
On a stormy night, Echoes? 'Call of the Drum!'
Tum ti tum titi tum, tum ti tum
Come Along, Bonnie Lads, Come Along
We need you, Bonnie Lads, Come Along
Bend an oar, Bonnie Lads, Come Along
Tum ti tum, titi tum, tum ti tum
The Call to the 'Zetland' on a snare drum.

A Quinn

WINTER WONDERLAND

In this winter wonderland,
Children walk hand in hand!
They play in the street and plan to meet!
Where they can sing and eat.
Where they can laugh and shout
And never have a doubt.
They'll have smiles on their faces,
In all of these places.
The joy they bring when they sing,
The bright lights shine and people dine,
Sitting in a chair, with all your Christmas fayre.
Laugh and be happy all the time
And you'll see the rhyme.
Loving and caring always sharing,
Christmas cheer with lots of food and beer.
No more tears and fears,
A New Year we start,
With hope in our heart.

Carol A Packham

WHERE EAGLES DARE

Oh! That I could float up on high
The sky to touch in a trance
And go forth onward through Heaven's length
Where eagles dare

Where are the birds of paradise?
Their wing tips covered with gold
Flying home to their Empyrean Isles
Where eagles dare

The point of departure on skyways unfurled
The sign of truth unbounded
Where the skirts of the dawn lay folded away
Where eagles dare

Sun-kissed feathers of albatross dust
Are all in the meridian true
Beyond the horizon, bound up in the blue
Where eagles dare

The lark ascending, his rainbow true way
As white bands are calling
In his maker on high he has placed his trust
Where eagles dare

Downward the great light is falling away
Like arrows of stealth are erasing
The scent of the seaweed is prompting a wish
Where eagles dare

The curtains of night abruptly are gracing
The azure which is fading to grey
The moon mist silently flows from the swell
Where eagles dare

Oh! Come now beloved to wonders so sure
As questions form wonderful answers
The glory of his love so grandly will lead
Where eagles dare

And when the Millennial Dawn comes to pass
And all the corals shine brightly
His good will shall send us at last to face
Where eagles dare

So Finally, Finally, Finally shall come
That peace that we so much desire
And lead us to a transcendent place
Where eagles dare

John London

ANCIENT ECHOES

Sound waves echo . . . echo . . . echo
Your call returns to you
Bouncing back and forth
A voice so clear and true.

Ringing out across the valley
Until a golden silence falls,
Rocky outcrops waiting
For another voice to call.

Come back . . . back . . . back
Don't leave me all alone,
A whispered echo . . . echo . . . echo
Emanating from ancient stone.

Christina Andrea

TIME TO CARE

Life can be too busy to always care
With hectic schedules making caring rare
Open our minds to the needs of others, and share
The troubles that can make life hard to bear.

Love thy neighbour as yourself, too
For this is an arduous and difficult task to do
Our time is precious and short to spare
Open up our hearts giving more time to care.

Like the good Samaritan, who did not walk by
Emulating the compassion and care, we can try
Filling our hearts with benevolence and love
And caring for humanity, as our Lord above.

Julia Keiser

HOPE

Why do deserts fourish as soon as the rains fall?
When we thought there was no life there at all,
It shows that many seeds had lain dormant in the ground,
Until the change of conditions let their lives abound.

It comes as a surprise when the land turns into green,
In a desert place where no life could be seen,
That life can be hidden or be difficult to discern,
It's a very important lesson for all of us to learn.

Maybe our lives like a desert have lain bare,
It may be that many seeds of hope lie buried there,
Seeds which are hidden, nowhere to be seen,
But could be developed into hope where despair has been.

Hope is what we require in our hour of need,
Hope is what we have when we are longing to succeed,
Hope is said to spring eternal in the human breast,
But hope by itself can only lead us on to second best.

Hope is not enough to ensure our success in life,
Hope by itself will not allow us to conquer strife,
We have to work at what our hopes require,
For there is no other way we shall fulfil our true desire.

Ron Martin

HANNAH MY DOG

Hannah was a puppy when we first met,
That moment was great I will never forget,
I got her for my birthday and I love her in every way,
Hannah loves me, it was so plain to see.
When she leaves me, I will be sad and down
But Hannah wouldn't want me to cry or frown.
Now she's gone, I'm all alone
And can't stop thinking of your first day home,
I love you Hannah and always will.

Tracy Salmon (14)

SIMPLE THINGS

Sometimes under a shade
I like to think aloud
How simple things make great things
How one small thing can make one large thing

How one sun ray and one rain drop
Can make a coloured bridge across the sky?
How one fish can keep a starving child alive?
So simple, yet so good

How can a gust of wind
Lead to a raging tornado?
How one man can destroy a building of pride?
So simple, yet so bad

How can love make people good?
How can love make people come together?
Love is so simple
So simple, yet so lovely!

Indresh Umaichelvam (12)

COLD BEANS AND WET SOCKS

It's raining again
And I'm stuck in my tent,
With a hole-filled ground sheet
And supporting pole - bent.
Swatting at midges
With my hands wracked with cramp.
As I attempt to find comfort
On a sleeping bag - damp.

The wind howls outside
Like a wolf at the moon.
Shaking thin canvas walls,
It'll find a way in, soon.
To nip at ten toes
Each cold, wrinkled and pink
Within wet, woolly socks,
Which, in a word - stink!

Two days have passed
Since I last saw the sun.
Then, my matches were dry.
It's not as it was - fun.
My cooker worked properly
And my bread grew no mould.
But now for tea, like yesterday,
It's a tin of beans - cold!

Paul Reynard

MEMORIES

Memories are not fictitious, but facts conceived in mind
  Not always is there beauty, not always are they kind
Like visions we have as children, they have a part to play
  In building up our future, fulfilling our each day

They give us so much pleasure, recording things now done
  Yet is so very different, with gifts for everyone
Those memories are the factors, embedded in the mind
  And dreams perhaps are fantasies, as in story books we find

Thoughts of our past childhood, vivid at times they seem
  Are treasured through the ages, not cast aside as schemes
Treasure those past memories, the good, the bad, the new
  For dreams are for the dreamers, and sometimes do come true

E F C Croker

BURGLAR BILL

I crept in the window, without making a sound.
I turned on my torch, and shone it around.

As quiet as a mouse, I made my way in,
Looking around, put money into my bin, (pocket)

I then turned my attention, to the rest of the house,
Creeping around, still as quiet as a mouse,

I opened the front door, so that I could get out,
A way to escape, if someone was about.

I then took the telly, a radio too,
Some rings and some jewellery, and their lucky horseshoe.

When they wake in the morning, they are going to feel ill,
For I've left them a 'thanks' note, from 'Burglar Bill'.

W J R Dunn

PRESENCE

Out of the window the stars shine bright
The snow is all around.
I whisper your name softly
And feel your presence near
I open my arms to greet you
And enfold you within.

Lady M

AWAKES TO SELBORNE

In beautiful rural Selborne, in East Hants there lie!

Vast unspoiled scenes; as seen in era gone by.
Village, parish, forest, farm meadow: all once cut by swathing scythe!
All viewed, admired from the magnificent, short and elongated
scenic Lythe,
Above on hanger, where beeches guard, so old and weather worn,
Far below, the village. In tranquil setting nestles old Selborne,
Now centuries old, no changes for the new, so very few!
Silent charm, where gentle village folk reside and their offspring grew,
Stroll the Zig-Zag to view the panoramic scene,
Of distant beauty, all hues and shades of green
Hedged by manicured maple, thorn, wild flora, butterflies too!
Slowly ascend upon the serpentine, to reach this perfect view.
Silent bugler, ravaged yew tree, tranquil graveyard trim and neat.
Green sloping meadow, with giant oak that shades, the summer heat,
And from the short onto the long Lythe great beeches stand so proud,
Rays; like gleaming swords; piercing through; hear avian sounds aloud!
The Wadden, near Wood Lane, the wishing stone on high,
The Wakes and Well-head, and White's walks beneath a clear blue sky,
Old Parish Ewe, the Plestor, the Peak, and Priories haunted plain,
Old blacksmith's shop, the village hall, a stroll down Huckers Lane.
Great Dorton, Grange and Gracious Street, De Gurdons, also Grimm,
Great house, now Norton's Farm where King and Queen stayed in,
Fishers' foray, Frensham pond, mallard, grebe and moorhen show,
Plantation, Seale, Oakhanger, trickle stream doth gently flow . . .
Mystical and elegant, the rural scene delights,
For the worldwide welcome stranger; who shows respect
at Gilbert White's
The naturalist who gave the world the feel for Nature's ways,
A gentle man of Selborne, and a life of happy days.
Oh where can peace of mind astound, to see wildlife at its play,
It's here in Selborne! Ancient England's pride portrayed,
It's here where past and present folk have lived with joy,
And most of all; have prayed!

William Johnson Lyth

A RESUMÉ

I went to France
to learn to dance
and returned
after my dollars I earned.

I went to St Francis
to join in all the local dances
but they sat around in trances
so I bid them farewell.

Soon after I left
I was brought to book
the policeman put me in a car
after he gave me a left hook.

I got three weeks remand
in court
but I tried to demand
that no charges be brought.

Towards the end of my stay in prison,
I caught a screw and a prisoner kissing
so I bonked him on the head
and went back to my bed.

I was amazed to see the woman judge,
wink, wink, nudge, nudge,
she asked me if I had a grudge
or did I want to see her fudge.

To cut a long story short
I got out and bought a bottle of port,
I went back to my little sort
and put on the kettle.

The kettle started up slowly,
I prayed to the most holy
and had a roly-poly
I switched on the telly and thought I was a goalie.

That goalkeeper for Arsenal,
we called him a grasser,
he had long hair and a brown beard,
He had a car that had just been geared.

Four years of my life
have just been rendered
and I have been tendered
by the opposite gender.

Frederick Lewis

SPRING

Spring is in the air
when lovers make a pair,
Lambs being born, and prancing on their way,
Flowers blooming opening their petals to the sun
Children playing together having fun,
Everyone feels younger, a swing in their step,
Oh how good it feels to be alive
thoughts of winter flying by,
Calming breezes instead of horrible winds,
Birds returning in the blue sky
singing their melodious songs,
Daffodils and crocuses blooming all around
Lawns being mowed, what a lovely sound,
Listening to the brooks flowing in the park
Maybe we'll hear the singing of a lark,
Easter's on its way in to show we care
visiting churches, kneeling in prayer
Remembering the rising of the Lord,
Oh if only these lovely thoughts would stay
instead of diminishing like clay.

M J Chadwick

9.11.01

Nine was the day
Eleven by many multiplied
One wink and all vanished away
So many injured and died.

Nine lives has a cat
Eleven by many multiplied
One strike and two went flat
On Wall Street there was nowhere to hide!

Nine some begin their daily chore
Eleven by many multiplied
One down together with many, many more
Who could have conceived this deadly ride?

Nine times I wondered why
Eleven times multiplied
One by one you did all die
After three years I still ask why.

Kareen Smith

A Spartacus In USA

I can't understand those people
whom I could say were a disgrace
For not giving safe protection
for those who improve the human race

Martin Luther King came from out of this background
and was assassinated for his stand
Although he knew he was a target
he never gave up his plans

He brought America to a standstill
when he withdrew the black man's labour
He did this without a gun being fired
which won him worldwide favours.

It is sad when one makes enemies
when improving the impoverished
Through distribution of wealth
to make life more civilised

There are far too many divisions
in our society today
Causing wars and terrorism
which are hard to chase away.

Lachlan Taylor

CLOSED TO DEBATE . . .

This person that I am
Is not really me,
For I am not as I appear to be.
At least not within my mind,
In there I could be blind,
For inwardly or outwardly,
I am not what I see.

I'm stuck in an image
I cannot rotate,
Nor am I ever able to decrease.
Yet I am all to well able to hate,
And distortedly overly increase.

I was never manufactured
To live in this shell,
I cannot bear to see its reflection.
Yet I repeatedly felt compelled to face the hell
Of the ritual of a mirrored inspection.

Do the scales ever lie?
Does the mirror deceive?
Neither, nor -
For they've no reason to try -
That's what I believe.

Controlled by distortion,
Controlled by weight,
Open to extortion
But closed to debate!

Louise Webster

UNTITLED

I can't explain the love that I hold for you in my heart
I feel it so strongly, it's tearing me apart
My love for you is endless, time will never heal
I do know deep inside, this is how I feel
The moment that I found you
I knew the bond was there
Our love for each other was never lost
The love that shows you cared
If wishes were horses I'd ride to you today
To feel your arms around me
To hear you say, 'Please stay'
But this can never happen, this will never be
Although you're in my heart
My eyes just cannot see
The angels took you from me
You had finished your time on Earth
But oh how much I miss you
I love you for all it's worth

Margaret Ward

Loss

Loss is sometimes the consequence
when affections are imprisoned in uncertainty
waiting for the perfect moment
that never seems to arrive.
An aspiration of the heart is easily thwarted
if living in the dawdle,
while life would have know escalation
whereby the two might live
happily ever after.

Carla Iacovetti

GONE AWAY

This August can't contain another May
Slipping through its fingers gone away -
Like breeze between the blades of corn now cast
Into the combine moving this way past

And as its day fades all the more to shadow
May to August seems to be a narrow
Portion of the lane it looks along -
Where light is fading and the clock hangs on.

Peter Asher

SHE'LL SURVIVE

Leaving home was on her mind as she walked out on him.
She knew she'd had enough of this, her life was looking grim.
No more lies, dread or pain, she'd given him her all.
Now she'd have a future, now she would stand tall.

Where would she go? She didn't know, nor did she even care,
As long as it was far enough for her to hide somewhere.
Her life had been a battlefield in which she'd never win,
But from this day her life would change, a new day would begin.

She'd left him lying in his bed sleeping off his drink.
He'd gone to sleep quite happy while his wife stood at the sink.
Doing everything she could for him both night and day.
No thanks, no love, no pleasure, she had to get away.

Walking through the darkness, feeling no regret or fear,
Her heart and soul felt lifted, she didn't shed a tear.
She'd never hear those words again, 'You're useless, you're a pain,'
Because she knew the truth now, this man was quite insane.

In the morning he'd call out for her to fetch his tea,
But no one would answer, she had broken free.
He'd go downstairs full of demands as every day he had,
Not knowing that she'd gone away, no more would she feel sad.

No more would she be used by him, or treated like a slave.
She'd have her independence, to her old life she would wave.
A long goodbye and smile again as she'd forgotten how.
She knew he'd miss her being there and he'd be lonely now.

Elizabeth McNeil

I WRITE A POEM EVERY DAY

And versify in every way
To suffer aspiration's loss
In wealth of adjectival dross.
Alas, I have the greater block
Of sleeping muse and waking clock.

I'm not an addict, just confined
To every verse, with hours defined
In days and nights; describing time
As life adrift in end line rhyme.
But mid-line lime, if tuned with gin,
Makes virtue of poetic sin:
To wallow in slow wave to hours,
In wakes of nights and bosky bowers
And precious rage for minutes lost
When love was weighed against the cost.

For nothing's ever what it seems,
The wanton days, the waking dreams:
Young nights described in minute form,
Of nightmares ridden in the dorm.
Old-age reprise, newborn in child-like bloom,
To light tomorrows of uncertain gloom
With no success in contests of the muse.

Eschew romantic poems; always use
Sick, sordid verse to fire the sure-fire shot.
Try trochee sagas, spiced with you know what:
Unsavoured sundown sung to tasteless thyme,
Arthritic rhythms in cold turkey rhyme.

Alan Chesterfield

WEAK FOR VIDEO

I am lost in these two spirals of madness,
of love, hate, death and laughter,
tales of sadness, loss and sadness,
stories of a king, a god, a martyr.

This is where my heart lies,
where my soul is found and lost,
when tears fill my eyes,
I ask, what does this passion cost?

When I'm old and dying,
when my fruit is drawn,
when my mortality is flying,
and I'm lost before dawn.

My fear is that this is my end,
sitting and eating,
not a single friend am I
meeting or greeting.

Because I am weak for video.

Josh Morrall

SNAPSHOT

Rosie sighs - she's closed the door
on polished step and gleaming floor.
Dishes washed and stacked up neat -
brand new slippers warm her feet.
Framed in the window she gazes out,
see cars and vans dashing about.
Small and wrinkled, with shawl and brush
she looks out on the daily rush.
With extra care through waist-long grey,
as it has done on every day,
the brush will soothe some of her woes;
her scalp tingles as it goes.
TV sits in the corner, shrouded by lace,
showing only a crescent of her weathered face.
Round stain on the polished wood -
will nothing turn again to good?
Where tea and fury both were spilled,
but all of value's been sold for bills.
The brush sweeps on with practised grace;
a rebel strand falls across her face.
She tucks it back with quick-flicked hand,
remembering the flash of twinned and tender marriage band.
Her friends on the sideboard in black-ribboned frames,
hold sepia smiles, push her into memories again.
Long dresses on the village green;
side parted hair alive with sheen.
A man smiles in a trilby hat;
was it so long ago as that?
And further back, in grim repose,
her father sits in Sunday clothes.
Her favourite frame flicked clean again,
she holds the picture in her brain.
They'd ridden miles in each other's arms,
she perched cheeky on the handlebars.

They'd stopped and drank and ate their fill
- when the world seemed not so ill -
and even canoodled under the trees;
she blushes still at the memory.
Then images invade still-born and red;
pale faces clustered around the bed.
No picture here of the son she lost -
with every breath she counts the cost.
Not a cry escaped his dry blue lips -
she'd barely touched his fingertips.
Empty-bellied and empty-armed,
poured grief and heart into husband's palms.
She sits and stares out at dull blooms,
eyes dark and veiled in misted gloom.
No one waves or taps on the window sill.
Familiar silence awaits the gentle kiss of the pills.

David R Smith

SUMMONSED BY THE DIVISION BELL

Vulgar is the team that works its set hubristic way
Its juniors fall, to safeguard seniors at their play:
Hoon is a saturnine, whose gloom of face reflects
Dark secrets that are walled up, this we must suspect
Jowell is the lady lacking *every* trace of guile
An independent BBC remains intact . . . awhile
Prescot barely holds himself in check
He would love to break each interfering journalistic neck
Reid is the Cerberus who gnashes teeth to guard the gates of Hell
He relishes the public's venom and their hatred far too well
The man of *Straw,* how his student radicalism lies buried, doubly dead
He preaches 'black is white', and critics? They are clearly off
                                                       their head
Clarke, that Cyclops, cannot be bearded in his den
Will the lure of book-burning ever be beyond his ken?
Blunkett is the one for whom the jury is still out
Whether it returns *at all,* there is the gravest, most judicial doubt
Hain claims to lead the house, but truth to tell
He serves his peers the less, his overbearing master far too well
For all, consistent are their statements, weasel-worded to the brim
For fear of failure and embarrassment, 'group-think' never is a whim
And finally: there's *Teflon Tony* at the helm
His virtues not just self evident, they are *designed* to overwhelm
The world against him, he'll never countenance another way
Who said that risible pomposity has had its day?
Soon, perhaps, the chamber's demographics will succeed
This zealot bunch be ousted, booted forth, and at full speed!
But wait: I see another on his subtle, mephistophelean way
He has the face of economics, knows the price to pay
and lies in wait for arrogant Icarus' fall
for *Brown,* that Scot-without-a-stain, *he* holds the future, all.

Chris Brookes

WISHES FOR MY CHILDREN

I wish for you my children,
That someday you all will find
A true and lasting happiness
Of the everlasting kind.

I wish for you my children,
That all your dreams come true,
And rainbows always follow you
In everything you do.

I wish for you my children,
That your troubles are far and few,
And you know that if you should need me
I will always be there for you.

I wish for you my children,
That contentment someday you will find
That you make old memories good ones
And leave any sad ones far behind.

I wish for you my children
Morning, noon and night
That all days are filled with sunshine
And your futures are always bright.

My final wish my children,
Is that someday you all will know
Just how much you all mean to me
And how I love you so.

Jan Cash

The Motorway

There is no beginning, there is no end
I see in the distance every single bend
3 lanes, 4 lanes, maybe 5
I concentrate fully to stay alive
Day and night there are always cars
The central reservation with its taut iron bars
This way, that way, what a hullabaloo
Stuck in a traffic jam on the M62
The humdrum sound lulls my ears
The AA man always allays any fears
Bridge after bridge, sign after sign
At last my slip road
Motorway, I resign.

Ivana Cullup

CHILDHOOD

Don't waste these childhood years
Don't try to grow too soon
You're in the morning of your life
Don't race yourself to noon
Don't pick a cross to bear
Enjoy yourself and play
For the pains of adulthood are not so far away
Show love for everyone
Before it is too late
And you begin to learn
That the world is full of hate
And when your childhood's gone
Please try to just remember
The experiences of spring
Must last you 'til December.

Robert Peirce

DECIDE IN THE EYES

I don't know about this, I'm not so sure
Then I look into your eyes, everything is pure
The Victoria Falls, forest of Nepal
Mount Everest, the San Francisco shore

I've climbed a mountain to reach the top
I'm not going to fall, like a waterfall drop
Hope is important, it keeps us on track
Once I've seen I shouldn't look back

I don't know about this, I'm not so sure
Then I look into your eyes, everything is pure

Perfect white snow on Christmas Day
A shiny new car, and you don't have to pay
Natural spring water, perfectly clear
Nothing sinister has ever been near

I don't know about this, I'm not so sure
Then I look into your eyes, everything is pure

Soon we'll be gone, we'll be taken away
At least though together, we're here to stay
Decide in the eyes, it worked for me
Open your own, then maybe you'll see.

Alex Harford

A SPLIT SECOND

Explosively to leave the blocks
And make a full-powered run
By a hundredth of a second
Can a race be won.

In qualifying heats
Still are race times reckoned
Fastest losers may get through
By a hundredth of a second.

Slow at the starting gun
May mean half a breath delayed
And in a hundredth of a second
Are new world records made.

The computer makes the measure
The computer only can
For a hundredth of a second
Is beyond the sight of man.

A hundredth of a second
The idea is absurd
Yet this may be the margin
Between the first and third!

Olive Cragg

BOGOF

The yellow sign stood out a mile,
And to my mouth did bring a smile,
An offer I could not refuse,
So many here from which to choose.

Bargains everywhere I see,
By buying one I get one free,
Something for nothing, a very good deal,
Providing me with an extra meal.

Was it money well spent?
As the food purchased was not my original intent,
Are consumers reaping a big reward?
That is if they can afford,

The extras placed into the trolley,
Making us fork out extra 'lolly',
We win, they win, who comes off best?
Let's put 'bogof' to the test.

What have you bought that was not on your list,
Just what was it you could not resist?
Ready-made meals, biscuits galore,
In your shopping trolley, half of the store.

I get so excited with cheese and ham,
Pasta, chicken and jars of jam,
I have decided that if 'bogof' is for me,
Then I will only take home the things that are free.

The items of food to be paid for,
I will leave behind in the store,
My cupboards will burst, my freezer brimming,
And with 'bogof' at last, I will be winning.

Ann G Wallace

DREAMCATCHER

Am I now too old to dream,
to hope and scheme
and weave my web of life from here,
am I as always held back by fear,
shaped by traumas and beads of tears,
my feathers clipped, dreams disappeared,
or is it time to change the scene
as ages wisdom pursues a bigger dream,
and as I weave with love each yarn of gold,
so other lives are touched by my stories told,
until, as my shaman teacher taught,
my dreamcatcher becomes a freedom tool,
not a web on which my spirit's caught.

Jean Caldwell

THE PELICAN

The pelican - who loves her young -
    To feed her hungry brood
Will tear her tender feathered breast
    And nurture them with blood.

By rationing their nourishment
    And feeding drop by drop
She manages to stay alive.
    Their hunger knows no stop.

If left to their own appetite
    They'd drink to satiation.
And the maternal pelican
    Die of exsanguination.

Valerie A Smith

RUINED

Carbon steel shuttering, iron grilles,
Supermarket trolleys in waters rills.

Burnt out cars near motorway links,
Chewing gum pavements in every precinct.

Bags of rubbish with nobody to collect,
Take-away garbage at every intersect.

Littered streets an absolute disgrace,
Graffiti towns with nothing left to deface.

It is in no war zone this filthy tide,
But amongst English might, English pride.

How could this malignancy have gained such a hold?
Rats out on the high streets, makes the blood run cold.

Car ashtrays are emptied in public places at leisure,
To see a lowly street cleaner would give such pleasure.

They are 'as rare as hens' teeth?' Do you agree?
We must reclaim our country. Beginning with you and me.

Mercy E Jackson

DESPERATE - LEE

Everything was done with speed, to wait seemed such a sin,
He rushed to school then rushed back home, Lee was getting thin.
In his speed he fell about, all day he rushed and ran,
So desperate to arrive was Lee, he collided with a van.
Now he lies in bed all day, two legs are sealed in plaster,
No way can Lee get on his feet, a snail can go much faster.
He calls for food no need to rush, can't run to do a wee,
Can't even cross his legs to wait, he lies there, desperately.
He knows it does not pay to fume, his lesson has been learned,
Now desperate Lee waits desperately, his bridges have been burned.
No more to rush, no more to speed; he lies there quietly,
With broken legs the desperate one, has changed to patient-Lee.

Doreen Roberts

OBSESSION

At first it didn't matter
Now it's a daily routine
It seems such a little thing
The obsession to be clean.

I've locked the doors
And checked the catches
The windows and the taps
The plugs and all the latches.

Turned off the TV, called in the cat
Taken off my shoes, emptied the bin
Cleaned the fridge, straightened the mat
What a proper mess I'm in.

Washed my hands, made the bed
Hoovered all around
I have this overwhelming need
To be totally house proud.

I've checked the door a dozen times
All the windows too
Even dusted everywhere
And disinfected the loo.

Now I sit and look around
Not seeing what I've done
My eyes are checking everywhere
Do I need a re-run?

Jacqui Beddow

THE FAMILY PHOTOGRAPHS

Up on top of Gran's old wardrobe, by her tea set kept for best,
I've come across a battered suitcase in the spare room kept for guests.

Packed inside are photo albums wrapped up tight against the air
preserving weddings, births and childhoods, carefully from
wear and tear.
Locked inside, the children's voices high-pitched laugh, in faded fields
see them skipping, dance in meadows - gangling limbs
and full cartwheels.

Long before the war was thought of children innocent of death
climbed up luscious English hillsides, flopping down to catch
their breath;
eyes alight with childish wisdom, summer sunshine in their hair,
playing games of knights in armour, rescuing their ladies fair.

Cameras then were Kodak boxes, 'Must stand still or it will blur!'
Mother pressed the liquorice lever, hear the click and shutter whirr.
Captured in the grainy photos, grinning out in black and white,
families of ragged children playing outside, day and night.

Here we see them now - all grown up, flapper dresses, shoes with spats,
gorgeous girls with deep waved tresses, long ago cut off their plaits;
handsome boys in jazzy waistcoats, hair slicked flat with Brylliantine,
arms around shy looking lasses, Edith, Iris, Joan and Jean.

I wonder if they saw war coming, sensed its looming shadows grow
over lives still bright with sunlight? Now I guess we'll never know.
Wait, I see the photos changing - formal portraits, sepia card:
so the war years are beginning; 'Toughen 'em up and train 'em hard.'

Still those grown up children's faces smiled, 'Just for the
camera please.'
Uniforms for all the young men, WAFS in skirts below their knees.
Smart they looked dressed up - but so young - not yet lost their
friends to war,
hopeful, happy, living, laughing, never had to fight before.

So the children in the suitcase went to war and didn't mind.
Most returned from wars destruction, others fate has left behind.
Sealed together in the moment, memories, ancestors past,
times of change, a world of H bombs, won a cold war peace at last.

Sometimes I hear the children's voices from the suitcase
                                    closed up tight,
families mixed up together, people's lives in black and white.
Up on top the old oak wardrobe, out of reach but not of mind
now the ones who lived before us live through photos left behind.

I'll end up in the suitcase someday, glossy colour, wedding smile
'Who's the redhead in the photo?' Then I'll live again awhile.

Joy Lewis

WHO UNDERSTANDS?

I don't understand the world, the way it is today.
Everyone, so full of self, nobody else, may have a say,
or voice their hopes, their needs, their fears,
no one else must laugh, or smile, mustn't show their tears.
It's 'I want this', or 'I want that', 'Come on, I want it now'.
No thought that someone, somewhere is wondering 'How?'
'How can I clothe my wife and kids? How can I pay that bill?
Too little money coming in, my family's guts to fill.'

Brian Muchmore

A BEAR'S HUG

Would you be me? I do think not
left out here alone to rot,
I once was loved by a lonely child
who turned to me when Dad went wild,
on certain nights I couldn't breathe
he'd hold me tight with such a squeeze,
but when he came into the room
out of his arms it's me he threw,
for a while the room was silent
it was that night he had been violent,
get up I cry to my keeper
let's run away . . . the silence deepens,
days go by I'm still on the floor
wanting my keeper more and more,
people come and people go
where is the boy that loves me so?
'Don't leave me here, come back,' I say.
We're meant to both be running away,
someone's coming into the room
no you're not him you're just a broom,
I've been swept up upon a heap
and he has gone to the stars to sleep.

Janette Fisher

ACROSS THE MILES

Miles apart, I miss you
Morning breaks, I want to kiss you.
Shall we ever see the dawn,
Feel the dew on misty morns?
Flowers opening
Shadows forming
I miss you.

Gillian Maynard

A SECRET GEM

This little town was once Saxon,
It really is quaint and so pretty.
Its full name is Bradford on Avon,
And it's close to a Georgian city.

The Spa Roman city's called Bath,
Eight miles up the river from here,
Reached by the old canal path -
Walk or cycle and stop for a beer!

Long boats and aqueducts you'll see
On the journey to this little gem,
Delighted you surely will be,
And you'll come here again and again!

Weavers cottages once filled with looms,
Packhorse bridges and ancient tithe barn,
Saxon chapels, medieval tea-rooms,
And craft shops round old Barton Farm.

So next time you visit the city,
Come also to this secret spot,
To miss it would be such a pity,
For we're sure you will love it a lot!

Philippa Howard

WHAT DO YOU THINK?

What do you think of the Bible?
Is it true for you?
Have all the people done what is written?
Do you have a view?

What do you think of the Bible,
Of all the written books?
Have they been food for thought
Making you have another look?

What do you think of the Bible?
Have you got tired of it yet?
Though you read a bit every night
Certain passages you don't get.

Keith L Powell

A RHYTHMIC OPERA

I once sat high above a hill, as sunlight lit upon a dale,
Encompassing that which was still, a young and beautiful female.
Oblivious to my secret gaze,
She took to dancing in the haze,
Where rabbits burrowed in the dark, beneath the soaring of a lark.

I watched her rhythmic opera, through curtains made of grassy stems,
That served to frame her elegance, reserved for bright encrusted gems.
The setting moved to grace the stream,
As she undressed to fill a dream,
Where darting minnows sought a chance, to play their part
                                                    in this romance.

The cooling water brought forth sighs, that set alight a fantasy,
As I delighted in her cries, I questioned her virginity.
Then watched the ripples rise and fall,
Upon her breasts, so pert and small,
As water lilies floated by, I slipped away and, don't know why.

Vernon Norman Wood

DREAMING!

If I possessed a looking glass
I would know what will come to pass
If I could see at dead of night
What is to be would come to light
If I had luck that favours me
I could plan my life more carefully
If I had the love of one who's near
Such might dispel this doubt and fear
If I had intuition keen
No more about life would I then dream
The will to live would be ensured
This present turmoil then endured
If I had a friend to stand beside
Behind my dreams I would not hide
Is there a way to see the 'light'?
Without the need for 'second sight'
To clear this fog make reality appear
To help others to me to endear
If my eyes could see consistently
Would I then live contentedly
If I could trust in He above
Would He share with me His precious love
To clear these dreams ridiculous
To out of life these thoughts to thrust
If you were I would you then see
It is mad to dream so ridiculously?
I am no seer - I cannot see
Please tell me how to act more sensibly
At last in He I see the light
Thanks to God I will be alright
I have climbed that wall and crossed that fence
I saw - I heard - I gained - common-sense!

Jon El Wright

THE HUSTLER

You claimed you'd never played before,
Had never held a cue.
You asked what was the difference
Between brown, pink and blue.

I explained all the rules that formed
The basis of the game;
Where the balls should be positioned
On the table for each frame.

You said you fully understood
What you had just been told;
And could we play just one quick game,
For peanuts, not for gold?

To me, that sounded fair enough;
Then you produced the sting.
You cleared the table at one go;
What chance had I to win?

I realised that I'd been 'had',
Been 'snookered', sure and true.
You made a monkey out of me,
But the peanuts are for you!

Brian M Wood

I WANT TO BE A POET

I want to be a poet
Whose verse will please all those who hear or read.
I want to be a poet
To stir passions, encourage and raise hopes of those in need.
I want to be a poet
Write about joy and love and what happiness it will bring.
I want to be a poet
Write about poverty, wealth, the man who would be king.
I want to be a poet
Write about history and visions of the future.
I want to be a poet
Write about good and evil, the wicked and the pure.
I want to be a poet
Write about King Arthur and his band of knights.
I want to be a poet
Write about everything and common sights.
I want to be a poet
Putting the magical word and phrase together
I want to be a poet
To dream my verse will be enjoyed forever and ever.
I want to be a poet
No one can convey everything, action, deed, love or disaster
                                        but I will try,
I will try, I will try until the day I die.

Terry Godwin

SWEETIE

I spotted her in the Rue de Paris
a neat little piece of confectionery
the frilly skirt floating just over her knees
was packaging, tempting and modelled to please.

Her roseate cheeks had the bloom of a peach
like fruit in an orchard that's just out of reach
a vision in garments that floated so free
the wrappings around her said, 'Hey! Look at me.'

Attention, attention she sought to invite
alluring and tempting like Turkish Delight
her lips freshly plucked from a red cherry tree
seemed to give out a message 'Please come, sample me'.

Like bright sugared almonds her beautiful eyes
just grabbed my attention like fondant surprise
that tempting young morsel, so pleasing to me
I saw from my wheelchair in the Rue de Paris.

Jonathan Bryant

GRIEF OF GOODBYE

The grey mountain road
Wends a crooked mile,
How many times I've wandered there
With net to catch your smile.

Lonely, is the air,
Over, is the sky,
Gone, beats my heart,
Our chance has said goodbye.

Summer was the sun,
Autumn mellowed leaves,
How can spring push through,
While winter still grieves?

Carol Ann Darling

SPLIT PERSONALITY

Love's hiding in the corner
  Hate's going out tonight,
He takes the knife and follows him,
  Itching for a fight.
He has no fear, drank too much beer,
  His gloved hand feels no chill,
Love's left behind,
  His half a mind,
      He's going out to kill.

Eltanto

KAREN

Dear Karen how much I miss you
You are so divine and loving too
I am always thinking of you
A lovely angel o so sweet
You really knock me off my feet
How I long to hold you tight
In my arms all of the day
And all of the night
Your love is a sheer delight
And everything is alright
Now we are in Heaven tonight
As the moon shines so bright
As your eyes sparkle
Like stars in the sky
As the clouds slowly pass by
When we kiss I can hear you sigh
As our hearts beat together
That is how it should be
A wonderful love for you and me
As the tree of life shines on us tonight
With a spiritual light
Shining so bright
As we hold one another so tight
We are in Heaven every night.

Gordon Forbes

MEMORIES OF THE PAST C 1916

It can be lonely growing old, however dear one's friends,
So many things one used to know have gone, though one pretends.
I'm glad I have so clear a sight, like pictures in my mind,
Of things I knew so long ago and never more will find.
The roadway where we'd skip and run when on our way to school,
The little park so green and quiet, that framed a little pool.
The cricket ground with mighty trees that surely foresters knew,
'Parr's Elm' they named the highest one - his ball above it flew!
Close by, the Trent was shallower, the 'ford' by which men crossed,
And still were seen some mighty beams although the bridge was lost.
The later bridge was wider far, to carry car or bus,
Horse-drawn they were in my young days, to 'town' they carried us.
They say the city's altered much, once Saxon fair, now black,
Not worse nor better, simply changed - O Robin Hood, come back!
Pretty and fair the girls one saw who walked the Market Place;
Well dressed, well shod, with dainty hands which shaped the local lace.
'Goose Fair', the ancient festival, which every autumn came,
For three days filled the Market Square - when moved, no
                                                more the same.
Oh you who share my memories, so few as years go by,
Give me your thoughts as I give mine - God's blessing on us lie.

Kathleen M Hatton

BOUNDARIES, BRICKS AND WALLS

Scotland, Ireland, England, Wales
Make up our prosperous land
My son is full of love for all
And with God we're hand in hand

Children are all quite the same
With hearts so full of love
Whether they are black or white
They're all from up above

We have to share our love out now
We have so much to share
We have to show all the world
For all children we so care

We've put up boundaries, bricks and walls
And seem to fear the 'other'
But deep inside your heart there's love
For every father and mother

The world is so much greater
The sea joins land to land
But only when we reach across
Do we touch 'another's' hand

Scotland, Ireland, England, Wales
Make up our prosperous land
We have to reach across the waves
So love is hand in hand

April Dickinson-Owen

BARBECUE

I'm out here in the garden,
I've sat out here for years,
No one ever bothers me,
Sometimes I'm bored to tears.
I like to sit and make up rhyme,
It always helps to pass the time.
Think of nature and the reasons
For the ever changing seasons.
Oh no! Another barbecue,
They've gone quite mad because it's new.
Oh look! The smell is in the air,
The smell of cooking everywhere.
Cars parking, dogs barking,
Music blaring, no one caring,
Eating, drinking, running around,
What a noise, that awful sound.
Children chasing in and out,
Stamping on the plants, no doubt,
If I could join in all the fun,
It wouldn't be so bad.
Instead I sit and watch them all,
It makes me feel so sad.
I wish that they would all go home,
So I could be here all alone.
I really want to have a doze,
When will it finish, goodness knows?
Thank goodness - now they've gone away,
Peace and quiet to end my day.
I'm glad that they have all gone home,
You see I'm just the garden gnome!

Hilary Ambrose

SIOBHAN FOR MUM

Hello Mum,
I know you've been trapped,
For a very long time,
Your energy sapped.
But it's never stopped us
From loving each other,
Me, your child,
You, my mother.
Thank you, for the times we had,
The memories are good
And I'm really glad,
That I have become
A mother too,
It's a privilege that,
I have shared with you.
Now your spirit at last is free,
I know you'll be watching over me
And I take my comfort,
From knowing this,
Your love is eternal
And sealed with a kiss.

Sue Umanski

HOPELESSNESS

The cold shattered mirror lies on the floor
Like some rugged terrain you can never cross,
Freezing, howling winds chafe skin raw
And self-esteem is an assured dead-loss.

Sucking on a lemon signals defeat,
The sharp venom leaves a bitter taste
And the odious stench from rotten meat
Builds the sad concatenate of life debased.

Like a boxer eyeing his nemesis
Before the grudge match has even begun,
Or a wounded animal *in extremis*
After the most futile, lung bursting run.

Derek Kempthorne

ABUSED

Run through smiles of dark intent
And squirm, caught in their vicious bite
Just as you think your screams are spent
Peace whispers, 'There is no respite'

From deeper shadows, faces loom
With eyes that burn into your soul
Alone within this chilling tomb
Escape seems far from your control

Flooding all your mortal senses
Fear decides your every move
The endless nightmare it dispenses
Your tormentor would approve

Heartbeat at the point of breaking
Help is nothing but a myth
Struggle with the breaths you're taking
Panic's reaching its zenith.

Kim Montia

UNTITLED

Knowledge is power someone stated
Thoughts of school I always hated
Out of my bed I had to be thrown
When I got there my mind turned to stone
Best days of your life they advised
Their kind words I always despised
Though now I know it to be true
So children take your cue
Make the most of your days at school
As knowledge is a powerful tool

Angela C Oldroyd

BATTERED LIVES

She awoke on the floor, all aching and sore,
The last she remembered, the last thing she saw,
Was a fist in the face, from the man that she loved,
Sometime before that, a kick and a shove.
It's all her fault, at least that's what he said,
Before he struck her, and left her for dead.
She dragged herself up, she was hurting real bad,
What had she done to make him so mad?
She must try to be good, and do all that she can,
Be a good mother, and love her man.
She washed her bruised face, not looking at all,
She then filled with fear, when she heard the front door.
'I'm sorry my love, it won't happen again,
I've bought you these flowers, I've been under some strain.'
Oh he is sorry, he loves me, I know,
If I give it more time, our love it will grow.
A few days go by, and everything's fine.
'Hello baby, had a good day? I've cooked us some stew.
I'll serve it now, if I may?'
'You call this food,' said her lover in hate,
Throwing the meal, as well as the plate.
She froze with the fear, of what he might do,
Her ending up with her face black and blue.
He grabbed at her throat, and tightened the hold,
She felt herself weaken, her blood running cold.
*'You're ugly and useless, clean up that mess,
And what are you doing, wearing that dress.'*
He threw her aside, she fell to the floor,
Gasping for breath, she saw her son, only four.
'Don't hurt my mummy,' said the boy, in a tearful cry,
'I will be better, I will be good, I will try.'
'Get out of here, before you get some.'
'It's okay baby, go to your room, go on run!'
The last thing she remembered, was a foot in the head,
Now she don't feel, 'Am I, am I, dead?'

She looked down, upon her own grave,
Seeing her son, oh he's being so brave.
'Oh my god, what have I done,
I've left my son, without a mum.'

Nikki Baxter

THREE O'CLOCK IN THE MORNING

Three o'clock in the morning,
Lying in bed wide awake . . .
Thoughts my mind keeps on spawning
Hardly much sense seem to make . . .
Memories of past adventures
Flick like a film past my eyes . . .
Now where did I put my dentures?
Tuscany must take first prize!
Dash it, that pain's there again.
Doctor says, 'There's little doubt
Nothing too bad, just a strain.'
Must take a pill, knock me out.
Did I pay electricity bill?
Meant to - will do so tomorrow . . .
That's today. I'm over the hill!
Think Georgina said she'd borrow
Car for shopping, so I'll walk
To station, 'twill do me good.
Must find time to have a talk
With senior staff about dead wood . . .
Try to make my mind a blank . . .
Counting sheep sends me round the bend . . .
Heard it said: 'Just walk the plank,
Sure to drop off at the end!'
Soon the new day will be dawning . . .
Must have sleep, full day ahead . . .
Feeling tired, can't stop yawning . . .
Aaaaahh! Think

    I'll

     just

     . . .

Geoffrey Matthews

PITY

Pity we almost loved
Always you remain above
Looking on with tearful eye
Touch of sorrow in your smile

I prayed, but couldn't become
Threads of my mind, loose and undone
Purity could not relate
To my repeated, fallen state

Shame we did not uncover
Root of all sisters and brothers
Sharing fear or Earthly despair
Waiting for love, only pity was there.

Simon Kilshaw

YOUR SOUL

There's a place you can go
Peace and calm you will feel
The feeling is magic
And time just stands still
You can meet yourself
And love you will feel
Tranquillity like never before it's so real
You can do what you want
And you will feel whole
Just close your eyes friend
For that place is your soul

Tracy Telfer

ODE TO POLYHMNIA

Over the top, is all this noise,
Neighbours from hell, with musical toys,
Mono, stereo or quadraphonic,
So what do they do with just one flick?
Shatter the peace, assault my ears,
This noisy attack; forced to hear,
Earplugs for use, or cotton wool,
Mind-numbing racket, a brain too full
Of tasteless sounds that mock the best
Composers who passed acid test;
Remembered for a thousand years!

Not forgotten, would laugh and jeer,
At these pathetic miserable wretches,
One week wonder that never stretches
Beyond the bounds to eons long,
Millenniums, the music strong,
A legacy for future age,
Time will tell, just ask the sage,
Immortal muse, I love you all,
Stand up proud, you braved a fall.

C Thornton

LOVING ME

I've been on this diet as long as I can remember
well, if I'm being honest I started in 1992, December
two pieces of celery, and plenty of water
I'm sure I'm drinking rather more than I oughta

hungry all day, gasping for some fat
forget about the hunger pangs by doing 400 crunches on the mat
stretch, two, three, four, five, six, seven, eight
this keep fit lark is something that I do hate

on the treadmill trying to run at least a mile
my legs are aching but I still raise a smile
maybe a sign of madness but I'm thinking of when
I can fit into the new dress I bought, the figure hugging size ten

on reflection the newspapers and mags are the ones to blame
putting all women into a 'small' category, saying we should
                                          all be the same
my thighs are big and so are my hips
I'm a full-bodied woman who has had enough of the water
                                          and celery sticks

Pass me the assorted chocolates, quick, quick, quick
but that doesn't mean that only fat passes my lips
36-24-36 I am not
I am finally happy with what I've got.

Bisi Akinola-Arutoghor

BRUISED AND WOUNDED

Bruised and wounded in the heart . . .
Not knowing how it came to start . . .
Pointing many fingers of blame . . .
In this hideous kind of game . . .

Bruised and wounded in the heart . . .
Unable at times to share my thought . . .
Desiring love and peace which I long had sought . . .
My heart has been rebuffed, trampled down . . .
With little or no tenderness to be found . . .

Bruised and wounded in the heart . . .
A gaping hole is realised . . .
What matters most is not the size . . .
But, closing the wound, is what healing needs . . .

Bruised and wounded in the heart . . .
Healing will come . . .
I sit and sigh as time passes by . . .
In many hours of watching flowers . . .
They are unaware of many needs . . .
Keeping busy . . . shedding their seeds . . .

Carol Olson

THE FIRST AND LAST MORNING

On the morning that I was born
I came to Earth on a unicorn.
Its silver mane starts to glow
We flew over lands of sun and snow.
On the morning I wore my first sock
I had a playmate of a huge roc.
To me in a strange tongue it did speak
There was a gold leaf in its beak.

On the morning I first started school
I went with an angel so very small.
It knew my every single thought
And made me win at every sport.
On the morning of my teens
I had a visit from some Pearly Queens.
Together we all done the Lambeth Walk
In the London tongue I started to talk.

On the morning I first got old
I found myself a real leprechaun's gold.
It was dropped from a flash rainbow
And the good and bad things it did show.
On the morning that I do die
Back to Heaven on Pegasus I will fly.
And in this astral bar I have a date
God and my family at the gate wait.

Colin Allsop

KITCHEN CAPERS

(For Bronnie)

A bustling Mrs Beeton I
With culinary plans,
Orchestrating percussive sounds
With noisy pots and pans.

I favour the nouvelle cuisine -
The menus I adore,
Using ingredients fresh and new
From my organic store.

My kitchen is a studio,
For cooking is an art,
So masterpieces I create
Are in a class apart.

I'm expert with a rolling pin
And wield it with a flair,
Rolling pastry with touch so light
It floats up in the air.

When I prepare a gourmet tea,
My Georgian trolley groans
With gateaux and profiteroles
And clotted cream-filled scones.

It's not just what you cook, but what
You call it when it's done.
Say tarte au pommes for apple tart.
In French it sounds more fun.

Celia G Thomas

APPEAL TO A LAX HEAD (IN HAIKU VERSES)

No, we've never met -
Yet we are street intimates:
Wits diametric.

I encounter you
Who parade in our town zones,
Clones of your image.

With this laisser faire
Beware the final outcome:
Some rule is needed.

You are the linchpin
In the whole community,
Pre-shaping parents.

And, are you school-proud,
Endowed with Doct'rate ideals -
Zeal's inspiration?

Don't plead peer pressure
(Measure of tart and sloven)
Govern by model.

Impose punishment
Meant, not merely empty threats:
Debts to be settled.

Your premises once
(Response to firm discipline)
In hindsight: pristine.

Eileen Ellis-Whitfield

MY JOURNEY

Travelling from Machynnletia to Stockport on the train,
Listening to my CD walkman, music pounding in my brain
Watching the scenery pass me by,
Absorbing the breathtaking beauty,
Being able to capture the invigorating flavour of the countryside.
Deed reds and effervescent greens,
Valleys, hills and trees,
The eye roaming as far as you can see,
Train on the tracks, winding and weaving through
Patchwork of fields that belong to this great nation,
All the while travelling to my appointed destination.

Janette Dann

THE ODYSSEY (ORIGINALLY BY HOMER) IN SONNETS

Odysseus was the leader of the bubbles (bubble and squeaks = Greeks)
Who went away to have a go at Troy,
If someone was required to sort out troubles,
It seems Odysseus was just the boy:
His wife Penelope, he left in Ithaca,
With Telemachus too, his baby son,
The Trojans were the ones he had to knacker,
Odysseus fought the war that must be won:
The Trojan leader's name was Menelaus,
His wife was Helen, a very tasty bird,
Her lover Paris said, 'They'll have to slay us
Before we'll ever part!' - He gave his word:
But when they'd beat the Trojans and gone home,
Odysseus was left there on his own.

Odysseus was fancied by a nymph named Calypso,
To her isle of Ogygia she lured him,
Hermes flew there because he was equipped so,
To get Odysseus released, as the gods had abjured him:
Athena paid a visit to young Telemachus,
And found Penelope's home over-run with rough suitors,
They were draining her wealth, taking her for a jackass,
And saying, 'If you think you can, execute us!'
Athena told Telemachus his dad was OK,
And one day very soon, he would return,
Telemachus was pleased, and prepared for the day
These parasites their lesson would learn:
Penelope refused to marry anyone else,
For Odysseus she'd patiently wait on the shelf.

Telemachus decided to go looking for his dad,
A friend called Peisistratus went with him,
They never told Penelope, in case it made her mad,
At Menelaus' Palace, they were told, 'Come in!'
A feast was being held and they were welcomed in and fed,
It soon became apparent who they were,
Telemachus found his dad was still alive, not dead,
On Ogygia Island, so he'd have to go there:
Calypso wasn't keen to let Odysseus go back home,
But Zeus sent Hermes saying, 'Let him go!'
She couldn't defy Zeus, and make Odysseus her own,
She helped him build a boat, and of her help made quite a show:
Poseidon caused a storm that wrecked and sunk Odysseus' ship,
He made it to Scheria - not scheduled on this trip.

Odysseus dragged himself ashore and quickly fell asleep,
He was found by Princess Nausicaa and her maidens,
They rescued him and clothed him, having saved him from the deep,
And took him to the palace, where with presents he was laden:
King Alcinous and Queen Arete asked him had he journeyed far?
And he told them his sad and sorry tale,
They promised they would help him on his way to Ithaca,
And promised him a ship in which to sail:
With Odysseus, Princess Nausicaa had now fallen in love,
And hoped that he would stay with her for life,
This happy land of Phaeacia was like Heaven up above,
And Nausicaa hoped to be Odysseus' wife:
Odysseus was asked to tell of all the paths he'd travelled,
So to his happy audience, his story soon unravelled.

Odysseus had been at the battle for Troy,
He and his men raided the lands of the Cicones,
When they left, a storm tossed their ship like a toy,
They got to the land the lotus-eaters called home:
Some men ate the lotus and soon lost their minds,
Odysseus did not eat the narcotic plants,
He rescued his men who had not seen the signs,
Then they went to the Cyclops, the fierce one-eyed giants:
The Greeks were all captured and kept in a cave,
The Cyclops ate some of the Greeks bye-and-bye,
Odysseus sought plans how his men he could save,
He blinded the Cyclops with a stake through his eye:
Polyphemus the Cyclops was Poseidon's son,
So Poseidon the sea-god was wild when he knew,
He savaged the Achaians with storms thereupon,
And so, to the Isle of Aeolus they flew:
The King of Aeolus gave Odysseus a gift,
Control of the winds, so his journey was swift.

The ship was not too far from Ithaca and home,
When the crew opened Aeolus' leather-bagged gift,
The winds all escaped, and a storm was thus blown,
Back to Aeolus' Isle they did shift:
Aeolus was not pleased to see them all back,
So he banished them all from his isle,
Without any wind, all the crew had to row
'Til they felt all their muscles would crack,
Their ships were attacked by the Laestrygonians,
Who sunk all but one in a while:
In one ship they got to the Isle of Aeaea,
Where Circe the Goddess did dwell,
Odysseus sent half of his men with Eurylochus
To see what the island did hold,
Eurylochus returned with a tale of woe and announced
He had not done too well,

Circe had changed all the men into swine, according
to the story he told:
Odysseus, armed with a magical herb, went off to rescue his men,
When he threatened Circe, she lifted her spell,
and the swine became sailors again.

Odysseus must sail to Hades, the sorrowful world of the dead,
He needed to consult Teireseus, a prophet to guide him back home,
He sacrificed there a black ewe and a ram,
and into a trench they both bled,
The spirits were drawn by the smell of fresh blood,
and out of Hades they had flown:
The blind seer Teireseus drank some blood first,
then he told of the perils to come,
The first was the Sirens who lured men to doom, they Scylla
and Charybdis as well,
If Odysseus could bypass these perils, then next came the
Cattle of the Sun,
Scylla was a 6-headed monster, Charybdis the whirlpool from Hell:
The monster grabbed six men and gobbled them up,
as they steered round Charybdis by feel,
The rest arrived at the island where sun-god Hyperion kept his cattle,
The sailors followed Eurylochus and killed some sacred
cows for a meal,
This angered the gods, so Zeus sent a thunderbolt that crashed so,
it made their teeth rattle:
It was then that Odysseus escaped to Ogygia, the island Calypso
called home,
So ended the story he told the Phaeacians of how he first came
to their home.

With a ship and provisions, Odysseus left to endeavour at last
to get home,
He was grateful for all of the generous gifts of King
Alcinous of Phaecia,
The magical ship carried Odysseus back, and he swore he would
never more roam,

He was happy at last as he stepped on the shore of his very own
island of Ithaca:
The goddess Athena met him on the beach, and got him disguised
as a tramp
So no one would see him and know who he was, and spoil his desire
for a fight,
The suitors who sniffed round his wife Penelope would think him
a beggar, a scamp,
His son Telemachus returned and they met and they plotted and planned
through the night:
The hatred and loathing they felt for the suitors, they saved every bit
that they'd got,
Odysseus was still in the clothes of a beggar, so no one would see
through his disguise,
Until he was ready to unload his venom, the suitors would then
cop the lot!
Still disguised Odysseus meets his wife, he and Penelope make a plan,
The suitor who can string Odysseus' bow, and shoot an arrow through
12 axe-heads will he her man.

Two faithful old servants, Eumaeus and Philoctious are in on the plan
with Telemachus,
As the suitors try to string the bow, the servants lock the door
to prevent any mass escape,
Odysseus claims a try and strings the bow and shoots an arrow
through the 12 axe-heads and kills the two ringleaders
Antinous and Eurymochus,
He then reveals his identity and his jape:
Telemachus and the two servants guard the way out and block the door,
Odysseus continues to shoot the suitors who have so upset his wife,
When there are no arrows left, Odysseus joins his 3 comrades
and they stand as an army of four.

The fighting ends when the four comrades are the only signs of life:
Reunited, Odysseus and Penelope make love all through the night,
The goddess Athena delays the sunrise to make the night time last,
Their love has withstood all the years of absence and still shows
their decision to marry was right,

After all each has gone through, their devotion still stands fast:
Odysseus reunited with his father Laertes, and when
the suitors' families attack,
Zeus intervenes and forces a peace pact and thus
they are all driven back.

Mick Nash

Footnote: Homer wrote 'The Odyssey' as a Greek epic poem. All translations have been written in prose. I hereby reclaim it for the world
of poetry.

LIFE

Our fate is sealed
but have no remorse
as that road leads on
to an unknown course
it could contain
pure delights
wondrous mysteries
within our sights.

Have no qualms
where fate leads to
let that path
enlighten you
we cannot delve
in this sphere
but with each new dawn
it will become more clear.

Rhoda Starkey

WAR

United Nations across the world
Thrown into evil darkness
Racism, poverty, religious discrimination.

Lost in the depths of despair
Destruction and fear
Empty souls, mindless
Blind to their own failures.

The world is torn in two
Buildings reach the sky
Generations fall victim
To the blackness that surrounds them.

Will we ever be at peace?
Torment, agony, pain and suffering
Are now part of our lives
We drown in the blood of our fellow men.

Sheena Harris

WHAT MAKES A WOMAN THE LOVELIEST LADY IN THE WORLD?

Could it be the female body with all those lovely curves?
Could it be her sexy bum that attracts all the males?
Could it be the size of her breast that attracts all the males?
No, even a farmer's daughter may have those lovely curves but does
she walk like a lady?

In my book the female body comes fourth

Could it be a beautiful face but they always say it's only skin deep?
Could it be the sparkle in those lovely eyes or could it be
the devil in her?
Could it be the cute turned up nose or is she really stuck up?
No, there's some nasty women that look beautiful.

In my book the beautiful face comes third

Could it be the attractiveness in her face that's not quite beautiful?
Could it be the coy smile she has when she looks at you?
Could it be the sexy eyes she has when she looks at you?
No, but we are getting very close now.

In my book the attractiveness in her face comes second

So what is the loveliest part of a beautiful lady?
Well it is the female body with all those lovely curves
And a beautiful face that's not only skin deep
Also the attractive face perhaps with that coy smile.

But with these you still need something more

For it's the brain that is the loveliest part of a beautiful lady
The brain makes all those lovely curves walk like a lady
The brain makes all the beauty in a face beautiful with softness
and kindness
The brain makes each movement you make and the gentleness
of your voice into

The loveliest lady in the world.

Yes if you have a beautiful brain that brings happiness
and love to whoever you meet
That doesn't ask for riches or jewels herself, then this lady
becomes the richest jewel in the world
You can be an ordinary woman or an attractive woman
but with a beautiful brain

You are the loveliest lady in the world.

Keith Jackson

HAPPINESS

Eyes of liquid azure
shine happiness on me

Mouth of soft red roses
smile happiness on me

Arms of warm embrace
spread happiness on me

Hips of moist seduction
churn happiness on me.

Simon Martin

CULLING GUNS IS NO ANSWER

Don't touch me!

You mould me to perfection, cradle and caress me.
You fondle and finger, but you don't impress me.

I am an extension to your manhood.
I have served you well.
Now you wish to dump me.

Who is she? Is she sexy like me?
Why won't you listen? Why won't you see?

I can't control your insatiable urge,
Now I'm a victim of this mindless purge.

It is not often you hear me complain.
I could not stop the brute of Dunblane.

Although you banned me, I meant you no harm.
But when mad men abuse me, I may lose my charm.

S Farley

LIVE FOREVER

This is a story of a friend of mine
He was always full of beans he lived life to the full
He lived for today and not thinking of tomorrow
He lived it so fast life and soul of the party twenty-four seven
He loved his cars and bikes and friends and family
And most of all his women
His nomadic lifestyle was made for him
He lived so fast and died so young
We never had a dull moment with him
He may have died but he will always live forever in our
Memory until our dying day.

Geoff Beatty

Midnight Sunlight

In the midst of the night,
The sun still shines bright,
As if it were a globe of fire,
Of warm and royal hearty desire.

While the sun goes down,
The moon rises to its dark high throne,
Just for today,
The midnight sunlight shines to portray,
A bright yellow bouquet.

Sophie Peppercorn (13)

WORDS

There are words we say in anger,
There are words we say to care,
But you don't need words of reassurance
To know that I will be there.

There are words to say for guidance,
There are words we do not say,
But you don't need words of reassurance
To know I'll be here each day.

Now words have all got meaning,
For me this is so true.
Then there's only three which really matter,
And they are I love you.

Dawn Graham

MY SEIZURE

What went wrong I cannot say
It seems my mind just went away
At least the bit that's held in sway
When memories past come into play

My mind went blank (Nothing new?)
I had no idea who was who
Aware of nought - not a clue
No thought at all of what to do

And through the void these devils came
Surrounded by a fiery flame
All the time they called my name
'Come to join our Devil's game!'

As upon my bed I lay
I tried to hold their thrusts at bay
I said that I would never play
They danced a while and went away

Through this world of nightmare dream
I tore the night in silent scream
Things are never what they seem
There never was this devil's team

They said it was a kind of fit
A seizure was the gist of it
That brought about the gibbering twit
Free of thought and free of wit

Though I didn't know a thing
I'm glad the seizure didn't bring
The void to be a constant thing
And life is back upon the wing.

Ray Ryan

Your Special Year

You've watched the seasons
Come and go
Encountered many changes
With busy days
And quiet nights
Through all the different phases
Your family grown
Have children too
Life has been full and fair
You had your share
Of tears I know
Have memories oh so rare
Enjoy the peace
The years have brought
Relax without a second thought
Now all the things
You've done before
You still remember
That's for sure
The early mornings
Later nights
Have gone completely
Out of sight
But they were lovely busy days
Now on to yet another phase
Of love
And on to special times
Where thoughts are ours
When you're inclined.

Jeanette Gaffney

ARMISTICE

No one blew a trumpet
No one banged a drum
No one told the peasants
The war had just begun

A belly full of hunger
A heart full of tears
No one told the peasants
That this war would last for years

Someone lost a father
Someone lost a son
No one quite remembers
When the plough turned to a gun

Now the peasants do the killing
Their faces marked and pained
The women do the crying
Their children getting maimed

The slaughter was remorseless
With mortar and the gun
No one quite remembers
How this bloody war begun

Now the fields lie strangely quiet
With the battle won and lost
The business looks richer
But the peasant counts the cost

Dave P Reddick

THE SECRET OF HAPPINESS

Much more of being, not compulsion of doing,
A peaceful lifestyle courting and wooing,
Not so much owning, grabbing and having,
But more of a sharing, a giving, a loving.

Spreading some cheer on sad dismal faces,
The warmth of your heart in sincerest embraces,
Small surprise gifts when they are least expected,
Kindness inclusive with nobody rejected.

Small things in life make changes entire,
Simplicity's best if to joy you aspire,
The best things in life are simple and free,
Like I care for you and you care for me.

We've made our existence most complicated,
Filled it with objects, we're never satiated,
Things drive our lives, other people's criteria,
Our minds are controlled by possession bacteria.

Give of your best, spread sunshine, and smile,
For we're here on Earth for just a short while,
So all we can do to lighten the load
Is not just clear thinking, but wisdom's true gold.

Emmanuel Petrakis

AND SO THEY SAY

In the future so they say
Worlds of distant dreams
Making life from other days
In stiff decay bringing delays
Around China town you know
Or in the book and in the grave
Wisdom and the new day
Yells aloud distant drums
And bands swinging into tune.

M Trainor

INFORMATION

We hope you have enjoyed reading this book - and that you will continue to enjoy it in the coming years.

If you like reading and writing poetry drop us a line, or give us a call, and we'll send you a free information pack.

Alternatively if you would like to order further copies of this book or any of our other titles, then please give us a call or log onto our   at www.forwardpress.co.uk

Anchor Books Information
Remus House
Coltsfoot Drive
Peterborough
PE2 9JX
(01733) 898102